The
Farmers' Market
Cookbook

by
Bruce Carlson

**HEARTS 'N TUMMIES
COOKBOOK CO.**
**3544 Blakslee St.
Wever, IA 52658**

A dinky division of Quixote Press

1

It was almost a mystical experience......that of planning to organize the cookbook around the various growing seasons. I was going to have it contain, first, recipes appropriate for the very first farm market goodies to come along.

Then, there would be a section of recipes using fruits and veggies that came along later in the season; followed by goodies commonly available in the early fall. Finally, I'd have a section for those things like late apples and pumpkins that come on so well just when the year is closing down.

It was going to be Oh-so-impressive! Folks would Oh! and Ah! just walking near the book......they would be so impressed.

Just about then, reality set in. What about those items available that farmers trade from places more northerly or southerly? And, what about the recipes that call for items that mature at different times of the year? Should I put those recipes under summer stuff or fall stuff?

I was whining about my problems to the office cat, and noticing that my voice was rising and my hands were getting clammy.

Cricket gave me that look that only a cat can give, and continued to wash his left hind foot.

Well, I wasn't born yesterday. I knew that was that cat's way of telling me to forget that whole messy way of organizing the book. So, I did, and here 'tis.

That is one dang smart cat.

3

I know you wouldn't be interested in a fundraiser for your group that's risk free and about as work free as you can get. I know you wouldn't want somethin' to use for a fundraiser that'll also promote folks shopping at farm markets. So, I'm not gonna even mention how you could use this book, or a customized version of this book to raise a bunch of money.

I know you'd rather work your heart out, fixin' goodies in a hot kitchen so you can sell the stuff to each other to raise a few bucks.

But, sometime, when you're slaving away in the kitchen . . . . . the idea of raising some money the easy way might flit across your mind.

If that happens, give us a shout at 1 (800) 571 2665.

So, why shop at a Farmer's Market?

Wow, there's lotsa reasons!

How about the fact that you'd have to follow the farmer out into the field to get things any fresher? Most times, the goodies in the market got up just about the same time you did that morning.

And, the prices.....you can't beat 'em. There's all sorts of middle men who aren't there when you buy from the farmer. Usually, he keeps some of that middle man money for his extra work, and passes the rest on to you as a savings.

An' another thing.....the man or gal who grew the food knows more about it than most folks, and can give you hints on how to store it, and how to fix it. He or she is proud of what he does, and is more than happy to talk.

The dollars you spend at the Farmers Market will circulate throughout the community, doing the local economy lots of good.

And, finally, if you have any kids....taking them along to the market is a great way for them to learn that carrots come out of the ground and apples come from a tree. That's a revolutionary thought to lots of kids, ya know.

DEDICATION . . . . .

. . . . . to all those hard-working folks who grow our food.

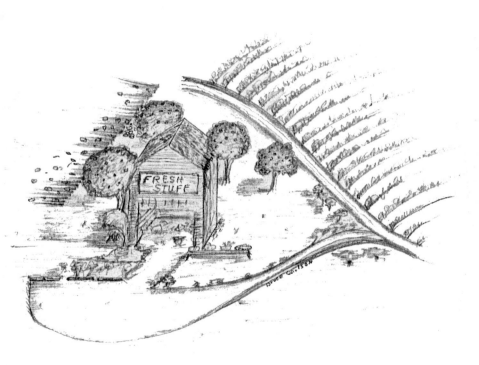

Appetizers & Beverages

APPETIZERS & BEVERAGES

STRAWBERRY ICE CREAM

1 qt. light cream
1 c. sugar
¼ tsp. salt
2 c. mashed ripe strawberries
½-1 tsp. vanilla or almond extract (optional)

Bring cream almost to boiling point, stir in sugar and salt. Add berries (if necessary, sweeten) and flavoring (the flavoring brings out the fruit flavor). Freeze. Should serve six generously.

Garnet Punch

¼ cup instant tea   2 cups apple juice
2 cups cranberry juice   1 quart lemon-lime soda

Place the tea in a punch bowl, add cranberry and apple juice, stir until tea is dissolved. Refrigerate. Just before serving add lemon-lime soda.

EASY FRUIT ICE

4 c. berries (raspberry or strawberries, fresh)

2 c. sugar
1¾ c. water
1 tsp. lemon juice

Mash berries, mix in sugar and let stand for one hour at room temperature. Force through a fine strainer. Add a very small amount of salt, the water and lemon juice. Freeze in refrigerator freezer (or in hand cranked freezer). Makes one quart.

11

QUANTITY FRUIT PUNCH

3 quarts pineapple juice
1½ cups lemon juice
3 cups orange juice
⅓ cup lime juice
2½ cups sugar
4 28-ounce bottles
carbonated water

1 cup lightly packed fresh mint
leaves
1 pint fresh strawberries,
quartered

Combine juices, sugar and mint. Chill. Just before serving, add remaining ingredients; pour over cake of ice in punch bowl. Yields 75 4-ounce servings.

VEGETABLE PIZZA

2 cans crescent rolls
1 C. cream cheese
½-¾ C. mayonnaise
May add chopped ham

Chopped vegetables: onions,
cauliflower, broccoli, peppers,
carrots, olives, radishes,
tomatoes (not fully ripe)

Spread roll dough on ungreased jelly roll pan and bake until lightly browned. Cool and spread with mixture of cream cheese and mayonnaise. Top with vegetables and ham.

FRESH FRUIT BOBS

Bamboo spears used with hibachi or fondue, or can use plastic spears
slices of mandarin oranges, fresh strawberries, bananas, white grapes, etc.

Alternate pieces of fruit on spear, one to a person, or making several and putting out on a tray so people may help themselves to as many as they (or you) may wish to eat. On a summer evening or a simple dessert they are especially popular.

Sauce for dunking the fruit:

1 c. Kraft mayonnaise
1 c. Kraft brand marshmallow creme
1 tsp. grated orange rind
1 tsp. ground ginger

Blend all the ingredients together and place in serving bowl with the fruit for dipping or "dunking." This gingery sauce is excellent for fruit salads too.

SUGARED PECANS

1 pound pecans
1 egg
1 tablespoon water

1 cup sugar
1 teaspoon salt
1 teaspoon cinnamon

Dip pecans into a mixture of egg and water. Then dip into a mixture of sugar, salt and cinnamon. Bake at 250 degrees for 30 or 40 minutes.

Cucumber Dip

1 pint commercial sour cream
1 envelope dried onion soup

1 medium cucumber
(diced fine)

Add cream for right consistency.

13

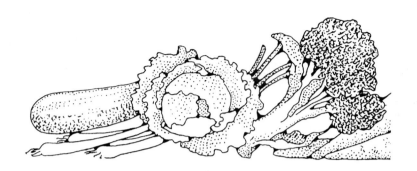

LETTUCE SNACK

1 pkg. crescent rolls
1 (8 oz.) pkg. cream cheese
1 pkg. Hidden Valley Ranch dressing

Shredded vegetables: lettuce, cucumbers, tomatoes, carrots, etc.

Roll crescent rolls out on a cookie sheet and bake until lightly browned; then cool. Spread cream cheese, mixed together with dressing mix, over the rolls. Top with shredded vegetables. Sprinkle shredded cheese over top. Cut in squares and serve. May use any vegetable combination desired.

HOT MULLED WINE

1 cup boiling water	12 whole allspice
½ cup sugar	12 whole cloves
1 lemon, sliced	4-inch stick cinnamon
1 orange, sliced	1 fifth dry red wine

In large saucepan combine the boiling water, sugar, sliced lemon, sliced orange, allspice, cloves and stick cinnamon. Bring to a boil. Reduce heat and simmer 5 minutes. Add the wine. Bring to boiling point. Do not boil, but simmer 10 minutes. Pour the hot mulled wine into thick glasses or mugs. Place a slice of lemon, a slice of orange and a few whole spices in each glass. Makes 6 to 8 drinks.

BAKLAVA

3 pounds chopped pecans	1 pound unsalted butter
3 teaspoons cinnamon	1 pound fillo (Greek strudel
2 teaspoons cloves	leaves)
1 cup sugar	

Combine pecans, cinnamon, cloves, sugar and mix well. Grease a 17½ x 12½ x 2-inch pan with melted butter. Place 8 filla in pan. Brush each with butter. Sprinkle top fillo with layer of nut mixture. Cover with 3 filla, brushing each with butter and sprinkling top fillo with nut mixture. Continue the 3-filla procedure until all nut mixture is used. Finish with 6 filla on top, brushing each with butter. With a sharp-pointed knife cut into small squares. Keep knife moistened with cold water to make cutting easier. Bake in preheated oven at 300 degrees for 1½ hours. Remove from oven. Cool and pour hot syrup over baklava.

SYRUP:

2 cups sugar	Juice of ½ lemon
4 ounces honey	2 or 3 cloves
1 cup water	1 teaspoon cinnamon

Mix all ingredients; bring to boil and pour over baklava. Makes about 2 dozen squares.

FRUIT WHIZZ

½ cup fresh fruit (banana,
  strawberries, peaches)
¾ cup skim milk
1 fresh egg
2 individual packages Sweet
  'n Low

1 tablespoon frozen orange juice
  concentrate
1 teaspoon vanilla
3 ice cubes, crushed

Combine the above ingredients in a blender; blend and serve immediately. Makes 12 fluid ounces. 225 calories per recipe. NOTE: Use Whizz as a meal substitute for 1, 2 or 3 meals a day.

HOT CIDER — SPICED

There's nothing like it.

½ gallon cider
½ cup brown sugar
16 cloves

1 tsp. allspice
1 tsp. nutmeg
2 sticks cinnamon

Heat cider and sugar to boiling point. Add spices and simmer for 10 minutes. Can be served cold, but it's better hot.

Hot Tomato Juice

6 cups tomato juice
1 can condensed consomme
1 teaspoon horseradish
1 teaspoon Worcestershire
  sauce

1 teaspoon grated onion or
  onion salt
Dash of pepper

In sauce pan, combine juice, consomme, onion, horseradish, Worcestershire sauce and pepper. Stud slices of one lemon with whole cloves and add to the juice. Heat just to boiling point, serve at once. Use lemon slices as floaters in each cup. Makes 8 servings.

Main Dishes

MAIN DISHES

18

19

Orange Glaze Sweet Potatoes

2 tablespoons butter
½ cup dark brown sugar, packed

1 orange, peeled and sectioned
3 cups hot, seasoned mashed sweet potatoes

Melt butter in skillet, add sugar and cook over very low heat until it bubbles, about 5 minutes. Add orange sections, simmer 10-15 minutes longer, until oranges look shiny and syrup thickens. Stir occasionally.

Spoon potatoes into warm serving dish and dribble orange mixture over top. Makes 6 to 8 servings.

Zucchini Squash Casserole

1 pound ground beef, brown slightly. Set aside in a bowl. In the skillet in which the beef was browned add 2 tablespoons fat and slice 2 small unpeeled zucchini squash. (Slice crosswise about ⅛ inch thick.) Add a small diced onion and cook about 10 minutes or until the squash begins to get tender. Add 2 cups of cooked (or raw peeled) tomatoes. Salt and pepper to taste. Simmer 5 or 10 minutes.

Into a 2 quart casserole put a layer of the squash-tomato mixture. Over this sprinkle a very thin layer (⅓ cup or little less) of uncooked rice. Add the browned ground beef and a little salt and pepper. On top of this put the remaining squash-tomato mixture.

Bake covered in 350 degree oven for 45 minutes. Uncover and place slices of processed cheese on top and bake about 10 minutes longer, or until the cheese has melted and browned slightly. Serves 6.

CAULIFLOWER SUPREME

1 head cauliflower	3 T. sugar
Salt to taste	Cheese slices
2 C. tomatoes	½-1 C. shredded cheese (opt.)
2 T. flour	1 small onion (diced or sliced)
2 T. water	Buttered cracker crumbs

Break cauliflower into pieces and cook with salt just until tender. Drain well then place in a buttered casserole dish. Bring tomatoes and onion to a boil in a saucepan. Make a paste of water and flour and add to tomatoes slowly. Cook until thickened. Add sugar. Pour sauce over cauliflower and top with cheese. Bake until cheese is bubbly and brown, 30-35 minutes, at 350°. Top with buttered crumbs last 5 minutes. (I like to add ½-1 C. grated cheese to vegetable mixture before baking.)

SWEET-N-SOUR ZUCCHINI

2 strips bacon	⅓ C. sugar (or 2 tsp. Sweet 10)
¼ C. diced onion	¼ C. vinegar
4 C. thin sliced unpeeled zucchini	Dash salt

Fry bacon until crisp, remove. Add onion, saute until clear not brown. Add vinegar and sugar. Add the sliced zucchini and bring to a simmer and cook until clear. Serve hot with bacon crumbled on top.

ZUCCHINI CASSEROLE

7 C. zucchini (chopped)	1 C. sour cream
½ C. onion	2 C. grated carrots
1-1½ lbs. hamburger	2 C. bread crumbs
1 can cream of chicken soup	2 T. butter

In a pan, combine zucchini and onion. Boil 5-10 minutes or until tender. Brown hamburger. Drain grease. Add soup, sour cream and carrots. Salt and pepper to taste. Combine zucchini and hamburger mixtures. Mix bread crumbs with butter. Put on top of casserole. Bake at 350° for 45 minutes.

CAULIFLOWER AND CARROTS

5 carrots (sliced, cooked)
1 (10 oz.) pkg. frozen cauliflower
   (defrosted)
1 small onion (chopped)

2 T. oleo (melted)
¾ C. milk
¼ lb. Velveeta cheese (grated)
½ tsp. paprika

Place carrots in bottom of baking dish. Next layer cauliflower over carrots. Mix together chopped onion, paprika, melted oleo, milk. Pour over vegetables. Sprinlke cheese over top. Bake at 350° for 37 minutes.

ZUCCHINI CASSEROLE

2 C. chopped zucchini
1 C. chopped celery
1 large onion (chopped)

1 can cream of chicken or
   cream of celery soup
1 box Stove Top stuffing

Put zucchini, celery and onion in casserole. Add 1 can cream of chicken or cream of celery. Mix 1 box Stove Top dressing according to directions and put on top. Bake at 350° for 30-40 minutes until done.

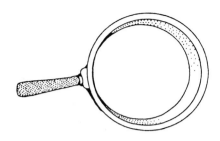

STIR-FRY VEGETABLES (Low Cholesterol).

1 tsp. cornstarch	2 C. broccoli (separated into
½ tsp. ground ginger (opt.)	flowerettes; cut the stems
1/8 tsp. garlic powder	into thin slices)
1 tsp. soy sauce	⅓ C. onions (sliced thin)
1 T. water	⅔ C. celery (sliced thin)
2 T. oil	1 C. bean sprouts
⅔ C. carrots (sliced thin)	(or use canned green beans)

Mix cornstarch, ginger, garlic powder, soy sauce and water in a glass measuring cup and set aside. Heat the oil in a large frying pan with a lid. When the oil is hot, add the carrots, onions and celery. Cook for 1 minute, stirring constantly. Then add the broccoli and cook for 2 minutes. Stir constantly. The broccoli will turn bright green. Add the liquid and continue cooking for 1 minute or until it's bubbly. Then add the bean sprouts, reduce the heat, cover the pan and cook for 2 more minutes. Serve over rice.

ZUCCHINI IN A SKILLET

1 medium zucchini (cubed)	1 large green pepper (diced)
1 tsp. salt	1 lb. hamburger (browned)
Flour (approximately 2 C.)	3 large fresh tomatoes
4 T. butter	Parmesan cheese
1 medium onion (sliced)	

Cut zucchini and coat with flour and salt. Brown in butter. Slice onions on top and saute. Dice green peppers. Add to above. Brown hamburger in another skillet and cut up fresh tomatoes and add to hamburger. Heat until tomatoes are warm. Combine ingredients from both skillets. Serve topped with Parmesan cheese.

CARROT RING

¾ c. milk
¼ c. soft butter or margarine
4 egg yolks
¼ c. flour
¼ c. onion
1 tsp. salt
½ tsp. pepper
½ c. diced cheddar cheese
1½ c. diced raw carrot

Blend above ingredients until vegetable is finely cut. Pour into saucepan, cook and stir over medium heat until thickened. Cool slightly and fold in 4 egg whites, beaten stiff. Turn into well greased ring, sprinkled with paprika, and bake at 325° for 50-60 minutes. Serve immediately. Good with creamed peas.

SAUERBRATEN

3 to 3½ pounds beef round or rump (boneless chuck roast)
1 teaspoon salt
½ teaspoon pepper
4 bay leaves
½ teaspoon peppercorns
8 whole cloves

2 medium onions, sliced
1 small carrot, minced
1 stalk celery, chopped
1½ cups red wine vinegar
2½ cups water
¼ cup butter

Rub meat with salt and pepper; place in deep earthenware crock or ovenware glass bowl; add bay leaves, peppercorns, cloves, onions, carrot and celery. Heat vinegar and water to boiling; pour hot over meat. Let cool. Cover bowl; refrigerate. Let marinate at least 48 hours, turning meat twice a day. When ready to cook, remove meat from marinade and dry with paper towels. Melt butter in Dutch oven and brown meat all over. Strain marinade and pour over meat. Cover tightly; simmer slowly 2½ to 3 hours or until fork tender. Remove to warmed platter; slice and keep warm. Serves 6.

GINGERSNAP GRAVY:

2 tablespoons sugar
1½ cups hot marinade
½ cup water

8 gingersnaps, crumbled
½ cup sour cream
¼ teaspoon salt

Melt sugar in skillet, stirring until brown. Gradually stir in hot marinade and water. Add gingersnap crumbs; cook and stir until mixture thickens. Add sour cream and salt to gravy; ladle some over sauerbraten and pass remainder. Yields 2 cups gravy.

STIFADO

3 pounds lean beef stew meat,
cut in 1½-inch cubes
1½ teaspoons salt
½ teaspoon freshly ground
black pepper
½ cup butter
8 small potatoes
6 small onions
1 6-ounce can tomato paste

⅓ cup red table wine
2 tablespoons red wine vinegar
1 tablespoon brown sugar
1 clove garlic, minced
1 bay leaf
1 small cinnamon stick
½ teaspoon whole cloves
¼ teaspoon ground cumin
2 tablespoons currants

Season meat with salt and pepper. Melt butter in heavy kettle with cover. Add meat and coat with butter, but do not brown. Arrange onions and potatoes over meat. Mix tomato paste, wine, vinegar, brown sugar and garlic. Pour over meat, potatoes and onions. Add bay leaf, cinnamon, cloves, cumin and currants. Cover potatoes and onions with a plate to hold them intact. Cover kettle and simmer 3 hours. Serves 8 to 10.

MUSHROOMS DIVINE

2 pounds fresh mushrooms
3 pounds onions, chopped
1 stick butter
1½ teaspoons salt

1½ teaspoons freshly ground
black pepper
Juice of 2½ lemons
Freshly ground nutmeg to taste

Wash mushrooms, but do not soak. Remove stems (freeze and save for soup or other use). Over low heat, saute onions in ½ stick butter. Place mushrooms, cap side down, on top of onions in large skillet. Fill cavities of mushrooms with pats of butter. Sprinkle with remaining ingredients. Cover and simmer about 12 to 15 minutes. Serve in chafing dish as hors d'oeuvres or as vegetable with steak or chicken. Serves 8 to 10 as a vegetable dish.

27

STUFFED BAKED POTATOES

4 medium to large potatoes
1 lb. pkg. California blend vegetables

½ lb. Velveeta cheese
Butter

Bake potatoes until done. Break open and butter. Cook vegetables according to directions. Spoon on potatoes and add slices of cheese, melt and eat!

POTATO PATTIES

3 medium potatoes
1 small onion
1 T. flour

1 egg (beaten)
1 T. milk
1 T. salt

Grate potatoes and onion. Add other ingredients. Mix well. Shape into patties. Fry in skillet.

FRIED TOMATOES

4 medium tomatoes (half ripe)
½ C. flour
2½ tsp. salt
2½ tsp. sugar

¼ tsp. pepper
¾ C. evaporated milk
Fat for frying

Wash tomatoes, do not peel. Cut in ¾-inch slices. Place on paper towels to drain. Combine flour, salt, sugar and pepper. Dust tomatoes on both sides with flour mixture. Add milk to remaining flour mixture to make a thick batter. Dip floured tomatoes in batter. Fry in hot oil until golden brown on both sides; drain.

SIDE RICE

1 medium onion (minced)
2 T. margarine

1 C. raw white rice
2 C. canned chicken broth

Saute onion in margarine. Combine onions, rice and broth. Bring to a boil; reduce heat and simmer. Cover 15 minutes or until broth is absorbed.

ZESTY GRILLED POTATOES

2-3 medium potatoes
¼ C. Italian salad dressing

½ tsp. salt
1/8 tsp. pepper

Heat 1-inch salted water to boiling. Add unpared potatoes. Cover and heat to boiling. Cook just until tender; about 30 minutes. Cut hot potatoes into ½-inch slices. Place in shallow glass dish. Pour dressing on hot slices. Let stand 1 hour, turning slices once. Remove potato slices and place on grill 4-inches from hot coals. Cook 8-10 minutes. Turn, sprinkle with salt and pepper on slices and cook until golden brown, 8-10 minutes.

OLD TIME SCALLOPED TOMATOES

3 C. home canned or store bought
   tomatoes
¼ C. butter
3 C. medium, coarse stale but not
   too dry bread crumbs

3 T. sugar
1/8 tsp. pepper
Dash of allspice

Heat tomatoes and butter in saucepan until butter melts. Mix in other ingredients. Bake at 400° for 40 minutes. Serves 4-6.

EGGPLANT CASSEROLE

1 eggplant
3 onions
1 stick margarine or butter
1 C. milk

1 C. shredded cheese
3 eggs (beaten)
1 tsp. baking powder
¼ lb. crackers

Cube eggplant; cut up onion. Cook onion and eggplant until tender. Drain and add margarine or butter, milk, cheese, eggs, baking powder and cracker. Bake in 350° oven until brown, about 1 hour. Put in layers of crackers, a layer of cooked eggplant, layer of cheese, ending with crackers on top. Mix milk, eggs, and baking powder and pour over all.

FRIED ONIONS

Large onions
1 egg
1 tsp. baking powder

½ C. milk
Pinch of salt
Flour (enough to make a thin
   batter)

Peel onions and slice evenly in ¼-inch slices. Make batter of the remaining ingredients. Dip slices of onion in batter. Fry in hot fat until golden brown. Serve with potatoes or fish.

TURNIP BAKE

Pinch of soda
6 large turnips (diced)
Cream or Half and Half

¼ C. sugar
1 T. flour
¼ C. butter

Cover turnips with water, add soda and bring to a boil. Drain. Cover with fresh water, salt to taste and cook until almost done. Drain. Put in 8x8-inch baking dish. Pour enough cream or Half and Half to almost cover. Mix sugar, flour and a little cream to make a thin paste. Stir into turnips. Dot with butter. Bake for about 1 hour in 250°-275° oven. Serves 8-10.

STUFFED PEPPERS

6 medium green peppers
1 lb. ground beef
2 T. chopped onions
½ tsp. salt

10½ oz. can tomato soup
½ C. grated cheddar cheese
Dash of chili powder
Dash of pepper
½ C. cooked rice

Wash and clean peppers. Brown hamburger, tops of green peppers, onions in skillet. Add ½ of tomato soup and cooked rice, cheese, chili powder. Stuff peppers, pour the other ½ of soup over peppers. Bake 1 hour at 350°. Freezes well before baking.

ZUCCHINI PATTIES

2 C. grated zucchini squash
2 T. grated onion
2 eggs (beaten)
A little salt and pepper

¼ c. grated Parmesan cheese
½ C. cracker crumbs
2 T. oil

Mix all ingredients together. Form patties. Heat oil in skillet. Cook patties 2 minutes on each side. Makes six servings.

ZUCCHINI AND TOMATO BAKE

4 medium zucchini (sliced)
½ tsp. soy sauce
¼ tsp. salt
¼ tsp. garlic salt
¼ tsp. pepper
3 T. oleo or butter

2 medium tomatoes (cut into wedges)
1 medium onion (sliced)
1½ C. (6 oz.) cheddar cheese (shredded)

Place zucchini in a 2½-qt. casserole. Sprinkle with ½ each of soy sauce, salt, garlic salt and pepper. Layer tomatoes and onions over zucchini. Sprinkle with remaining ½ of spices and seasonings. Top with cheese and dot with oleo. Cover. Bake at 350° for 40 minutes.

ZUCCHINI PATTIES

⅓ C. biscuit mix
¼ C. Parmesan cheese
1/8 tsp. pepper

2 slightly beaten eggs
2 C. shredded zucchini
2 T. butter

Mix all together until moistened. Drop by spoonfuls into hot greased skillet. (I add onions, chopped fine.)

SHRIMP JAMBALAYA

3 tablespoons butter or
  margarine
½ cup chopped green pepper
½ cup chopped celery
2 cloves garlic, crushed or
  minced
½ cup chopped onion
½ cup chopped green onion
¼ pound diced cooked ham
2 cups chicken broth
¼ cup chopped parsley

⅛ teaspoon black pepper
⅛ teaspoon cayenne pepper
3 large tomatoes, chopped
  (about 5 cups)
½ teaspoon salt
¼ teaspoon thyme
1 cup uncooked rice
3 4½-ounce cans shrimp or
  1 pound cooked shrimp
1 bay leaf
¼ cup chopped green pepper

Heat butter in large iron skillet over low heat. Stir in green pepper, celery, garlic, onions and ham. Cook over medium heat 5 minutes until onion is tender. Add chicken broth, parsley, black pepper, cayenne pepper, tomatoes, salt and thyme. Cover and bring to a boil. Add rice; stir with fork and simmer covered 20 minutes until rice is tender. Add shrimp, bay leaf and green pepper. Simmer uncovered 5 minutes. Makes 6 to 8 servings. Preparation time, 25 minutes; cooking time, 30 minutes.

SHRIMP CASSEROLE

1½ to 2 pounds cooked shrimp, shelled
2 10¾-ounce cans cream of shrimp soup, undiluted
1 large onion, diced
4 stalks celery, diced
¼ cup margarine
4 tablespoons sherry
4 hard-boiled eggs, chopped
2 cups cooked rice
8 ounces sharp cheese, grated
¾ cup buttered bread crumbs

Saute' onion and celery in margarine. Add shrimp, soup, sherry, eggs and rice. Pour into a 13 x 9 x 2-inch buttered casserole. Sprinkle top with cheese and bread crumbs. Bake at 300 degrees for 1 hour. Serves 8. For company, serve with steamed zucchini and a green salad. Homemade rolls add the perfect touch.

CHICKEN BREASTS IN WINE SAUCE

4 large chicken breasts, halved and boned
Salt
Pepper
¼ stick butter
4 tablespoons green pepper, chopped
2 carrots, finely chopped
1 cup mushrooms, finely chopped
2 small onions, minced
2 cups chicken broth
1 tablespoon flour
¾ cup white wine

Clean chicken breasts and rub with salt and pepper. Brown lightly in melted butter. Remove and place in buttered casserole or baking pan. Set aside. To the skillet in which breasts were prepared add green pepper, carrots, mushrooms and onions, sauteing approximately 5 minutes. Stir flour into chicken stock and add to browned vegetables. Continue to stir until sauce thickens. Season to taste and simmer 10 minutes. While sauce is simmering, pour wine over breasts and place casserole in a 350-degree oven for 10 minutes. Remove from oven; pour vegetable sauce over chicken breasts; cover and return to oven. Bake 1 hour or until tender. Serve with wild rice or saffron rice. NOTE: Consider adding an extra chicken breast per man for heartier serving. Serves 6 to 8.

CHICKEN AND DRESSING

1 large stewing hen or turkey
12 cups bread crumbs
1 cup chopped onions
1 tablespoon sage
1 tablespoon black pepper

1 tablespoon celery seed
½ cup sugar
4 eggs
Salt to taste

To make bread crumbs, bake a 10-inch pan of corn bread. Add enough cracker and light bread crumbs to equal 12 cups. Boil bird; cool; and remove from bone, reserving broth. Mix bread crumbs, onion, sage, pepper, celery seed, sugar, eggs and salt. Add enough broth for proper consistency, making thinner than desired. (It thickens as it bakes.) Bake until heated through and brown on top. Meat may be mixed with dressing or placed on top. If preferred, bird may be stuffed. Serves 12 to 15.

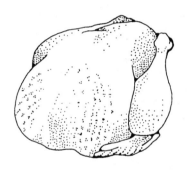

CURRIED TOMATOES

6 fresh tomatoes, cut in half
¾ cup mayonnaise
¾ cup sour cream

¾ teaspoon curry
Lawry's salt

Combine mayonnaise, sour cream and curry. Spread over tomatoes. Sprinkle with Lawry's salt. Place on greased cookie sheet. Bake in 350-degree oven for 30 to 40 minutes. Serves 6 to 8.

SUPER-DUPER POTATOES

9 medium-sized red potatoes
1 stick butter
2 cups half and half
1 scant tablespoon Lawry's
   seasoned salt

½ pound medium Cheddar
   cheese, grated

Boil potatoes (do not peel) until done (not mushy). Refrigerate overnight. Peel and grate potatoes on medium-sized grater. Set aside. Grate cheese and add to grated potatoes. Melt butter in pan; add half and half and salt. Mix all ingredients and pour into a 2-quart casserole dish. Bake covered in 350-degree oven for 1 hour and 15 minutes. Serves 8 to 10.

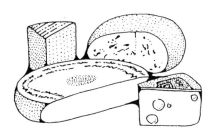

STIR FRY VEGETABLES

2 tablespoons butter
2 tablespoons oil
1 bunch carrots, peeled and
   thinly sliced
¾ to 1 pound mushrooms, thinly
   sliced

5 medium green onions with
   tops, thinly sliced
1 tablespoon lemon juice
¼ teaspoon salt
¼ teaspoon pepper

Heat butter and oil in wok or frypan until bubbly. Add carrots, mushrooms and onions. Stir and fry until crisp and tender, about 7 to 8 minutes. Stir in lemon juice, salt and pepper. Serves 8 to 10.

FAR EAST CELERY

4 cups 1-inch celery slices
1 5-ounce can water chestnuts
1 10¾-ounce can cream of
   chicken soup

¼ cup diced pimiento
½ cup soft bread crumbs
¼ cup toasted almond slices
2 tablespoons melted butter

Cook celery slices in small amount salted water for 12 minutes, leaving them still crisp. Drain. Add water chestnuts, soup and pimiento. Pour into 1½-quart casserole dish. Combine bread crumbs and butter and sprinkle over mixture. Top with almonds. Bake 1 hour at 350 degrees. Serves 8.

SHISH KABOBS WITH PEPPERS, ONIONS AND MUSHROOMS

12 ounces lamb
10 tablespoons low calorie
   Italian dressing

1 green pepper
1 onion
12 mushrooms

Cut lamb into 4 equal pieces. Divide each of these pieces into 6 equal pieces or cubes. Marinate lamb in low calorie dressing at least 6 hours. Boil peppers and onions 1 minute before placing on skewer. Alternate pieces of green pepper, onion, mushrooms and lamb. Broil on grill 7 minutes per side. Yields 4 servings with 333 calories per skewer.

CABBAGE ROLLS

1 head cabbage (medium)
1 medium onion (diced)
2 lbs. hamburger

½ C. rice (cooked and drained)
Salt and pepper to taste

Mix together hamburger, onion, rice, salt and pepper. Take ½ C. meat mixture, wrap in cabbage leaf. Repeat with all meat mix. Place in baking pan. Add ¼ C. water. Cover and bake at 350° for 1 hour or until done. If you like cooked cabbage, cut up remaining cabbage and place on top of rolls in baking pan.

SPINACH STUFFED TOMATOES

6 medium, ripe tomatoes
1 10-ounce package frozen
   spinach, cooked according to
   package directions
1 tablespoon green onion,
   chopped
1 tablespoon diet margarine

1 teaspoon Cavender's Greek
   seasoning
1 tablespoon horseradish
Salt and pepper to taste
½ cup dry bread crumbs
¼ inch water in baking dish

Sauté onion in margarine. Add salt, pepper, horseradish and cooked spinach which has been drained well. Core tomatoes and sprinkle insides with Cavender's seasoning. Stuff tomatoes with equal amounts of spinach mixture and sprinkle bread crumbs on top. Place in a greased baking dish with ¼ inch of water. Bake at 350 degrees for 30 minutes. Serves 6 with 85 calories per serving.

CORN CASSEROLE

½ C. onions (chopped)
½ C. green pepper (chopped)
¾ stick oleo
1 C. crackers (crushed)

Salt to taste
1 C. milk
3 eggs (beaten)
4 C. corn

Saute onion and green pepper in butter. Beat eggs and add crackers, milk, corn and salt. Mix well and bake at 350° for about 30 minutes or until golden brown on top.

BAKED ZUCCHINI

1 medium zucchini (cubed)
2 eggs
¼ C. sour cream
½ C. onion (chopped)

½ C. shredded cheddar cheese
Salt and pepper to taste
1½ C. buttered cracker crumbs

Boil zucchini in water until just tender; drain. Beat eggs slightly, blend in sour cream, onion, cheese, salt and pepper. Mix gently with zucchini. Pour in a buttered baking dish and top with crumbs. Bake at 350° for 35 minutes.

CHICKEN KABOBS

3 boned chicken breasts,
   cut in 1-inch chunks
1 8-ounce can diet pack
   pineapple chunks
3 medium apples, cubed
½ cup soy sauce
¼ teaspoon oil

½ cup water (or juice from
   pineapple and water)
1 clove garlic, minced
1 package Sweet 'n Low
¼ cup wine vinegar
¼ cup sherry

Combine soy sauce, oil, water (or pineapple juice and water), garlic, Sweet 'n Low, wine vinegar and sherry. Add chicken, pineapple and apple. Marinate for 15 minutes. Alternate chicken, pineapple and apple on skewers. Broil approximately 15 minutes, basting occasionally with marinade. Serve with marinade for dipping. Serves 4. 281 calories per serving.

PERFECT FRENCH-FRIED ONIONS

⅔ C. milk
1 egg
3 Bermuda or mild white onions

1 C. flour
Fat for deep fat frying

Combine milk and egg in bowl, beat well. Pour in shallow pan. Coat onions with milk mixture. Drop rings in flour. Fry (375°) until golden brown. Remove from fat and drain on paper towel.

CABBAGE FOR THE KING

2 C. coarsely chopped cabbage
2 tsp. salt
2 T. butter
1 T. flour

2 C. milk
¼ tsp. pepper
1 C. grated cheddar cheese
¼ C. buttered cracker crumbs

Cook cabbage with 1 tsp. salt in ¼ C. boiling water for 3 minutes; drain well. Melt butter in saucepan. stir in flour to make a smooth paste. Add milk, remaining 1 tsp. salt and pepper. Cook until thickened, stirring constantly. Arrange cabbage with white sauce in layers in a buttered casserole. Top with cheese and crumbs. Bake at 275° for 1 hour or until bubbly. (If you want to see your family change its mind about cabbage - try this!!)

SCALLOPED CARROTS AND CHEESE

12 medium carrots (pared and sliced
1 small onion (minced)
¼ C. oleo
¼ C. flour
1 tsp. salt
¼ tsp. dry mustard
2 C. milk

Dash of pepper
¼ tsp. celery salt
American cheese or Velveeta
cheese (10 slices ¼-inch thick)
3 slices bread (buttered and
cubed)

Cook carrots until tender; drain. Cook onion in oleo 2-3 minutes. Stir in flour, salt, mustard and milk. Cook, stirring constantly, until smooth. Add pepper and celery salt. Arrange layers of carrots and cheese alternately in a 2½-qt. casserole, ending with carrots. Pour sauce over casserole and top with bread cubes. Bake uncovered at 350° for 25 minutes or until cubes are golden brown. Serves 6-8.

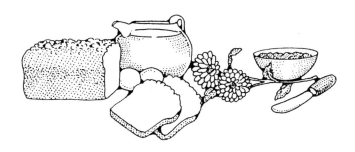

CARROT CASSEROLE

5 C. sliced carrots
½ lb. processed cheese
½ lb. margarine

1 small chopped onion
Crushed crackers

Layer carrots and cheese in a casserole. Saute onion in butter and pour over carrots and cheese. Top with crackers and bake at 350° for 30 minutes.

SCALLOPED CARROTS

4 C. carrots (cut up)   1 C. Velveeta cheese (cut up)
½ C. onion (diced)   1 stick butter
½ C. celery (diced)

TOPPING:
½ stick butter   12-15 crackers

Cook carrots, onions and celery in salted water until tender. Pour off water. Stir in cheese and butter. Put in buttered casserole dish. Then add topping. Melt ½ stick butter and add crumbled crackers. Spread over carrots. Bake at 350° for 20-30 minutes.

Bar B Q Hamburgers

2 pounds hamburger   4 tablespoons prepared mustard
1 onion   3 to 4 tablespoons sugar
1 green pepper (optional)   4 tablespoons vinegar
1½ cups catsup   Water to make moist

Simmer until thoroughly cooked. Addition of ¼ cup quick oatmeal will keep hamburger moist and help hold it together.

MEAT IN CABBAGE ROLLS

½ C. rice   1 C. milk
1¼ C. milk   2 tsp. salt
1 large head cabbage   ¼ tsp. pepper
1 lb. ground beef   2 T. brown sugar
¼ lb. ground pork   ½ C. hot water

Cook rice in 1¼ C. milk over low heat until fluffy. Remove cabbage leaves from head and immerse in boiling salted water, cook until partially translucent and pliable; drain. Combine meats with 1 C. milk, salt, pepper, and rice. Mix thoroughly. Brown rolls in hot fat, sprinkle with brown sugar, and water. Cover and cook slowly about 2 hours. Thicken broth for gravy.

BAKED TOMATOES

4 firm medium-sized tomatoes
Small amount of Jane's Krazy
Mixed-Up salt or Lawry's
seasoned salt
Small amount of seasoned
pepper

Small amount of garlic salt
Dried chives
Seasoned croutons
1 ounce grated cheese (Swiss or
diet Cheddar)

With sharp knife cut out cone-shaped opening at stem of tomato, large enough to hold small amount of ingredients. Sprinkle into each tomato liberal amounts of salt, pepper, garlic salt and chives. Top with grated cheese and 3 or 4 croutons. (If diet permits, a teaspoon of diet margarine may be added.) Place in shallow casserole with small amount of water in bottom. Cook about 15 minutes at 350 degrees or until tomato skins are crinkly. Serves 4. 61 calories each.

BARLEY PILAUF

"This dish takes some trouble, but is worth it,"

¼ lb. butter
½ lb. mushrooms
2 med. onions, sliced or chopped

1¾ cups pearl barley
1 quart chicken stock or 6
chicken boullion cubes

Heat in skillet 2 Tbsp. of the butter. Add mushrooms, and cook gently for 4-5 minutes. Remove mushrooms and heat remaining butter. Add onions and brown. Then add barley and cook slowly, stirring until it browns. Transfer barley, onions and mushrooms to casserole. Add chicken stock or cubes to one quart boiling water. Pour one-half of this over the casserole. Cover and bake 30 min. at 350°. Add last half of liquid and bake another 30 min. Uncover and bake about 5 min. more.

MEXICAN MEAT LOAF

So good and easy, it will make the whole family shout "ole."

2 lbs. ground beef	**1¼ cup tomatoes**
1 egg	**2 tsp. salt**
½ cup corn meal	**½ tsp. sage**
½ cup onion	**¼ tsp. chili powder**
½ cup green pepper	**dash tabasco**

Mix all ingredients. Put in a loaf pan and bake at 350° for 1½ hours.

ZUCCHINI OMELET FOR ONE

A delicious meal anytime, especially when served with fresh fruit.

2 slices bacon	**8 slices zucchini, ⅛ inch thick**
1 egg	**1 tsp. flour**
3 Tbsp. milk	**2 Tbsp. grated cheese**
salt and pepper as desired	

Fry bacon in small (seven inch) skillet. Remove bacon and all but one Tbsp. of the grease. Place slices of zucchini in skillet. Fry on one side. While zucchini is frying, beat egg, adding flour and milk. Add cheese and crumbled bacon.

When zucchini is brown on one side, turn and pour on egg mixture. Cook on slow heat until set. Loosen edges and turn out on a plate. This is delicious served with fresh fruit.

COUNTRY RIBS AND KRAUT

A dutch oven treat for all pork ribs fans.

1-1 lb. 11 oz. can (3½ cups) sauerkraut and juice	3-4 pounds loin back country ribs
2 unpared tart apples, sliced	2 tsp. salt
1 Tbsp. sugar	¼ tsp. pepper

Simmer ribs in water for 30 minutes. Drain and trim off fat. In Dutch oven, mix kraut, apples and sugar. Season ribs with salt and pepper. Place meaty side up over kraut. Cover and bake 2 to 3 hours at 300°. If desired, bake the last half hour uncovered to brown. Can add quartered potatoes last hour. Baste ribs and kraut with juices several times during last hour. Serve ribs, kraut and juices. Serves 4 to 6.

BRAISED BEEF SHORT RIBS WITH VEGETABLES

Number 2 choice in restaurants. Braised in oven, no watching necessary. Bake 325° for 2½ hours. Makes 6 servings.

5 lbs. beef short ribs, cut in serving size pieces	1 medium size onion, chopped (½ cup)
½ cup finely chopped celery	1 tsp. salt
1 cup finely chopped carrots	¼ tsp. pepper
1 can condensed beef broth	½ leaf marjoram, crumbled
1 cup water	1 Tbsp. flour
	2 Tbsp. water

Heat Dutch oven; rub fat edge of meat over hot surface to grease. Brown ribs well on all sides. Drain off fat.

Add onion, celery and carrot to Dutch oven; saute until lightly browned. Add beef broth, water, salt, pepper and marjoram. Return ribs to kettle; cover.

Bake in slow oven (325°) for 2½ hours, or until meat is very tender. Remove ribs to serving platter; keep warm.

Pour liquid from kettle into quart measure or bowl; skim off fat. Return liquid to kettle and bring to simmer. Combine flour with water, stir into simmering liquid. Cook, stirring constantly until sauce thickens and bubbles 3 minutes. Serve with ribs.

Small boiled potatoes, green beans and carrots or sauerkraut may be served with the ribs, if you wish.

FRENCH ONION RINGS

¾ C. flour
¼ tsp. salt
½ C. milk
2 T. oil

1 egg
3 medium Bermuda onions
1½-qts. vegetable
oil for frying

Sift flour with salt into bowl. Add milk, 2 T. oil and egg. Beat until smooth. Cut onions into ¼-inch slices and separate into rings. Dip each ring into the batter. Drain excess batter over bowl. Meanwhile place oil into cooker. Preheat at 425° uncovered. Gently place a few rings at a time into the heated oil. Do not crowd rings. Fry 5-6 minutes, turning occasionally. Drain on absorbent paper.

ONION PATTIES

¾ C. flour
2 tsp. baking powder
1 T. sugar
½ tsp. salt
Fat for frying

1 T. cornmeal
½ C. powdered milk
Cold water
2½ finely chopped onions

Mix dry ingredients. Add enough cold water to make a thick batter. Mix in onions. Drop by teaspoon into hot fat. Flatten patties. Fry to golden brown.

ONION RINGS

2 egg yolks
⅔ C. beer
2 T. oil
1 large onion

2 egg whites (chilled)
1 C. flour
1 tsp. salt
½ tsp. pepper

Beat together yolks, beer, oil, salt and pepper. Stir in flour. Mix only until smooth. Let stand 1 hour. Slice onions and separate into rings. Beat whites until stiff, then fold into beer batter. Dip rings into flour, then into batter. Deep fry to golden brown.

GOLUMBKE

1 medium cabbage
1½ lbs. ground beef
1 (15 oz.) can Spanish rice
1 tsp. salt

1/8 tsp. pepper
1 (1 lb.) can tomatoes (broken up)
½ C. water

Remove 12 cabbage leaves, trim hard center vein. Blanch in boiling water until softened, about 8 minutes. Combine meat, Spanish rice and seasoning; mix well. Spoon mixture into the center of each leaf. Fold sides over and roll up. Place seam down in a 9x13x2-inch pan. Pour on tomatoes and water. Cover, bake for 1 hour.

QUICK BEEF ORIENTAL

1 lb. beef round steak (½-inch thick)
⅔ C. water
1 (0.8 oz.) pkg. instant meat
 tenderizer
1 large onion (sliced)
1 medium size green pepper (cut into
 ¼-inch strips)
2 T. vegetable oil
1 (16 oz.) can bean sprouts (drained)

1 (4 oz.) can mushroom stems
 and pieces
2 T. soy sauce
1 tsp. instant chicken broth
¼ tsp. garlic salt
1 T. cornstarch
2 T. water
Chow mein noodles

Trim fat from beef. Cut beef into 2x1/8-inch strips. Mix ⅔ C. water and meat tenderizer in bowl; stir in beef. Let stand 5 minutes; drain. Cook and stir beef, onion and green pepper in oil in a large skillet over medium heat until beef is brown, about 3 minutes. Stir in bean sprouts, mushrooms (with liquid), soy sauce, instant chicken broth and garlic salt. Heat to boiling. Mix cornstach and 2 T. water, stir into beef mixture. Cook and stir until thickened, about 2 minutes. Serve over chow mein noodles. Makes 6 servings.

BEANS 'N TOMATOES

1 pt. green beans
2 tomatoes (chopped)
½ C. sour cream

¼ C. Italian dressing
¼ C. chopped onions

Cook beans and cool. Combine with onion and dressing several hours ahead of time. One hour before serving, mix in sour cream. Add tomatoes just before serving.

GREEN PEPPER STEAK

1 lb. beef chuck or round
(fat trimmed)
¼ C. soy sauce
1 clove garlic
1½ tsp. grated fresh ginger
or ½ tsp. ground ginger
¼ C. salad oil

1 C. green onion (thinly sliced)
1 C. red or green peppers
2 stalks celery (thinly sliced)
1 T. cornstarch
1 C. water
2 tomatoes (cut into wedges)

Cut beef into thin strips 1/8-inch thick. Combine soy sauce, garlic and ginger. Add beef. Set aside while preparing vegetables. Heat oil in large frying pan or wok. Add beef and toss over high heat until browned. Taste meat. If it is not tender, cover and simmer for 30-40 minutes over low heat. Turn heat up and add vegetables. Toss until vegetables are tender and crisp about 10 minutes. Mix cornstarch with water. Add to pan; stir and cook until thickened. Add tomatoes and heat through. Serves 4.

SHIPWRECK

3-4 lbs. ground beef (browned and
seasoned)
Sliced onion

Sliced raw potatoes
½ gal. size can kidney beans
1 C. uncooked rice

Layer the above in large greased roaster. Top with 1 (51 oz.) can tomato soup and enough water to cover. (Heat soup plus 1 can of water.) Cover and bake at 350° for 2 hours.

GARDEN HASH

2 cucumbers (quartered and cubed)	½ tsp. celery seed
2 grated carrots	½ C. vinegar
1 green pepper (chopped)	½ C. sugar
1 onion (chopped)	¼ C. oil
2 tomatoes (cubed)	

Mix vinegar, sugar, oil and pour over vegetables and refrigerate several hours or overnight. No salt or pepper (makes soft).

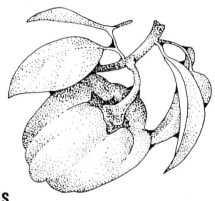

SKILLET SCALLOPED POTATOES

4 C. raw potatoes (sliced)	1 C. milk
3 T. butter	½ tsp. salt
1 onion (chopped)	1/8 tsp. pepper
1 C. boiling water	

Put butter in large skillet. Add sliced potatoes, onions. Cook and stir 3-4 minutes. Add water, milk. Cook 30 minutes. Stir often.

ONION RINGS

1 C. flour	1 T. vegetable oil
1 egg	1 tsp. baking powder
1 C. milk	Sliced onions (1½-inches to
¼ tsp. salt	2-inches in thickness)

Sift flour, salt and baking powder. Add egg, milk and vegetable oil. Mix well. Dip onion rings into batter and deep fry in hot oil until golden brown.

47

SCALLOPED CORN

2 C. whole kernel corn
1 small onion (diced)
1 C. diced cheese
1 pkg. Escort crackers (crushed)

1 egg (beaten)
⅔ C. milk
Buttered cracker crumbs

Mix corn, onion, cheese and crushed crackers. Beat egg and add milk. Combine both mixtures in greased casserole dish. Bake 50 minutes at 350°. Top with buttered cracker crumbs and return to oven until browned.

CHEESE AND POTATO CASSEROLE

6 medium potatoes
8 oz. shredded Velveeta
¼ C. butter or margarine
2 C. sour cream

⅓ C. chopped green onion
1 tsp. salt
¼ tsp. pepper

Cook potatoes in skins until well done. Shred like hash browns. In large saucepan melt butter; add cheese until almost melted. Add remaining ingredients except potatoes and stir. Add potatoes and stir lightly. Place in buttered casserole and dot with butter. Bake 25 minutes at 350°. Freezes well. Lasts several days in refrigerator. Reheat 30 minutes at 350°.

PARTY POTATOES

10 medium potatoes (cooked and
   mashed)
8 oz. pkg. creamed cheese
Butter to dot top

1 C. sour cream
2 T. chives
Salt and pepper

In large bowl mix all ingredients and put in a 9x13-inch buttered pan. Cover tightly and refrigerate until 1 hour before serving. Bake 1 hour at 350°.

48

ZUCCHINI ROUNDS

⅓ C. Bisquick
¼ C. Parmesan cheese
1/8 tsp. pepper

2 slightly beaten eggs
2 C. unpeeled shredded zucchini
2 T. margarine

Stir together Bisquick, cheese and pepper. Add eggs and fold in zucchini. Melt margarine in skillet. Use 2 T. of mixture for each round. Cook 2-3 minutes on each side until brown. Makes 12.

SALT-FREE MEAT LOAF

1 lb. lean ground beef
¾ tsp. allspice
¾ cup applesauce

2 Tbsp. chopped onion
1 egg, beaten

Mix, pack into loaf pan, pour topping over, and bake at 350° for one hour.

TOPPING:

1 apple, cut in rings
1 tsp. dry mustard

¼ cup brown sugar
⅛ tsp. cloves

Press apple rings on top of meat loaf. Mix other ingredients and sprinkle over top.

STUFFED PEPPERS

4 large or 6 medium peppers	½ tsp. salt
1 lb. hamburger	½ cup chopped green peppers
¼ diced onion	1 egg beaten
½ cup diced celery	½ cup rich milk

Cut tops from peppers and remove seeds. Combine rest of ingredients. Mix well. Fill the peppers with mixture and place in shallow baking pan. Cover with Creole sauce as follows:

2 cups cooked tomatoes	¼ cup diced onion
½ tsp. salt	1 tbsp. sugar
½ tsp. cinnamon	1 tbsp. flour
6 whole cloves	¼ cup water

Combine first 6 ingredients in sauce pan and cook gently for 10 minutes. Strain. Mix flour and water and add to above stirring and cooking until thick. Pour over peppers and bake at 350 degrees about 40 minutes. Pepper may be parboiled and stuffed as follows:

1 cup minced ham	2 tbsp. flour
1 cup cooked rice	2 tbsp. butter
1 tbsp. chopped onion	1 cup milk, dash of salt

Mix together the ham, rice and onion. Make a white sauce of flour, butter and milk. Combine the two mixtures and stuff the peppers. Sprinkle with buttered bread crumbs and bake gently for 35 minutes.

CHOO-CHOO SANDWICH

1 loaf French bread	Cheese slices
¼ cup butter or margarine	Thin slices corned-beef loaf
1 clove garlic, minced	Green pepper rings
Tomato slices	

Cut bread diagonally in 1½" slices — not quite through bottom crust. Cream butter with minced garlic. Spread on bread slices. Place tomato slice, cheese slice, corned beef slice and green pepper ring between bread slices. Bake on baking sheet in moderate oven 350° 20 min. or stick skewer through loaf lengthwise; wrap in foil; place on grill. Turn frequently. Heat until cheese melts. Cut through bottom crust just before serving. Makes 7 to 10 servings.

GRILLED POTATOES

Potatoes (unpeeled)	Salt
Butter	Pepper

Slice washed and dried potatoes lengthwise about ½" thick. Butter each one generously. Sprinkle with salt and pepper. Fit slices together again. Wrap each potato in heavy duty foil. Place on grill and bake about 40 min.

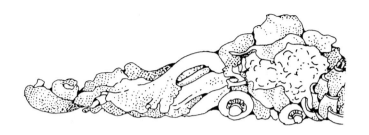

Salads

SALADS

COLE SLAW

1 medium head cabbage
and carrots, green peppers, celery
or any other veggies you like
½ C. sour cream
¼ tsp. salt

½ C. salad dressing
½ C. sugar
1 T. vinegar
½ tsp. celery seed

Chop fresh veggies and mix well. Add other ingredients. Slaw will keep 2 weeks. Dressing amounts can be doubled if head of cabbage is large.

CAROLINA COLESLAW

1 large cabbage (3 lbs.)
1 large green pepper
1 large sweet Bermuda or Spanish
onion
1 C. sugar

1 tsp. dry mustard
1 tsp. celery seed
1 C. cider vinegar
⅔ C. vegetable oil
1 tsp. salt

Trim, quarter, core and grate cabbage. Core, seed and mince green pepper. Peel and chop fine onion. Toss vegetables. Bring dressing ingredients: sugar, salt, dry mustard, celery seed, cider vinegar and vegetable oil to a boil. Pour over cabbage and toss well. Gets better and better the longer it sits in refrigerator.

COLE SLAW

1 medium head cabbage
1 small onion
¾ C. sugar
1 C. vinegar

1½ tsp. salt
1 tsp. celery seed
1 tsp. prepared mustard
¾ C. oil

Shred medium cabbage (5-6 lbs.) and small onion. Cover with ¾ C. sugar. Let stand. Prepare 1 C. vinegar, 1½ tsp. salt, 1 tsp. celery seed and 1 tsp. prepared mustard. Bring to a boil. Add ¾ C. oil and bring to a boil again. Pour over cabbage and onion. Let stand at least 24 hours. Will easily keep 2 weeks. Cut ingredients in half unless for large group.

GERMAN POTATO SALAD

1 lb. bacon (diced, fried and drained)
¼ C. vinegar
1 C. water
1 T. (heaping) flour
Bacon drippings
Salt and pepper to taste

½ C. sugar
5 lbs. potatoes (cubed and cooked)
1 large onion (chopped)
6 hard boiled eggs (chopped)

Mix flour into bacon drippings. Add vinegar and water. Stir over medium heat to a gravy consistency. Stir together all remaining ingredients. Pour vinegar mixture over all and toss together. Serve warm.

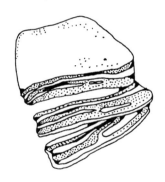

HOT POTATO SALAD WITH BACON

2 lbs. potatoes (sliced)
¼ C. chopped onion
⅓ C. bacon drippings
¼ C. vinegar

1 T. sugar
½ tsp. paprika
¼ tsp. salt
6 slices bacon

Cook potatoes in salted water until tender and drain well. Fry bacon and drain on paper towel. Saute onion in bacon drippings until tender. Stir in vinegar, sugar and seasonings. Mix lightly with potatoes and bacon. Serve warm.

REALLY POTATO SALAD

3 medium potatoes
2-3 eggs (hard boiled)
½ tsp. prepared mustard
½ tsp. sugar

2 sweet pickles (chopped)
1 stalk celery (chopped)
3 T. mayonnaise
1 T. vinegar

Mix all but eggs. Add chopped eggs. Stir lightly and chill.

SUMMER SALAD WITH TUNA OR SALMON

1 head of lettuce
Cooked macaroni (amount your choice)
1 green pepepr
Onion (if desired)

1 large can tuna
About 3 tomatoes
1 large cucumber
Mayonnaise

Toss all together.

SHRIMP PASTA SALAD

2 cans tiny or medium deveined
   shrimp
2 lb. bag shell macaroni
1 small stalk celery (diced)
4 hard boiled eggs (diced)
1 large jar mayonnaise
Large tomatoes
Lettuce leaves

1 small jar pimento (drained)
1 large onion (diced, opt.)
1 large carrot (finely diced)
1 tsp. salt (opt.)
1 tsp. fine ground pepper
1 tsp. lemon juice
1 tsp. mustard (opt.)
Paprika

Drain shrimp and rinse. Put shrimp on ice or in ice water at least 30 minutes before combining with other ingredients. Cook macaroni until tender. Drain and blanch with cold water. When macaroni is cool combine with all remaining ingredients except tomatoes. Mix well and add more mayonnaise if consistency is too thick. Drain shrimp and mix into salad. Cover and refrigerate overnight. Quarter tomatoes (do not cut all the way through). Set tomatoes on lettuce leaf and spoon in shrimp salad. Sprinkle lightly with paprika. Serve cold with salad crackers. Serves 8-12.

GAZPACHO SALAD

1 cucumber (peeled and sliced)
2 tomatoes (chunked)
1 red onion (cut in rings)
Sliced mushrooms (as desired)

3-5 boiled eggs (sliced)
1 green pepper (cut in rings)
Strips of Swiss cheese

Mix together and season with seasoning salt. Dress with Italian dressing.

MARINATED PASTA AND VEGETABLE SALAD

2 C. uncooked macaroni (cooked as directed, rinsed and drained)
½ C. vegetable oil
¼ C. ReaLemon lemon juice
¼ C. water
1 pkg. Italian salad dressing mix

1½ C. small broccoli flowerettes
1 C. coarsely shredded carrots
1½ C. sliced zucchini
¼ C. chopped green onions
⅓ C. grated Parmesan cheese
Lettuce leaves (opt.)

In cruet or small jar with tight-fitting lid, combine oil, ReaLemon, water, and salad dressing mix; shake well. In large bowl combine all ingredients except lettuce; toss with dressing. Cover; chill several hours or overnight, stirring occasionally. Serve on lettuce, if desired. Refrigerate leftovers.

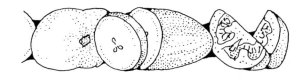

GARDEN PATCH PASTA SALAD

2 C. elbow macaroni (uncooked)
2 C. zucchini slices (cut in half)
½ C. red pepper (chopped)
8 bacon slices (cooked and crumbled)
3 hard boiled eggs (chopped)
1 tsp. dried oregano (crushed)

½ tsp. onion powder
½ tsp. pepper
¾ lb. Velveeta (cubed)
¾ C. mayonnaise
3 T. milk
2 tsp. prepared mustard

Cook macaroni according to package directions; drain. In large bowl combine macaroni, zucchini, red peppers, bacon, eggs and seasonings. Mix lightly. In saucepan combine Velveeta, mayonnaise, milk and mustard. Stir over low heat until cheese is melted. Combine with macaroni mixture, toss lightly. Chill 3-4 hours, stirring occasionally.

CAULIFLOWER SALAD

Large head cauliflower (cut in small
  pieces)
1 C. shredded cheddar cheese
¾ C. mayonnaise

1 envelope original Hidden Valley
  Ranch dressing mix
1 C. sour cream

Mix dressing ingredients and toss together with cauliflower. Grate more cheese on top if desired.

ITALIAN VEGETABLE SALAD

8 medium green peppers
  (cut in strips)
6 cucumbers (sliced)
16 C. tomatoes (chopped)
4 medium onions (thinly sliced)

8 T. or ½ C. red wine vinegar
½ C. salad oil
4 tsp. basil
2 tsp. salt
1 tsp. pepper

Mix green peppers, cucumbers, tomatoes and onion together. Combine wine vinegar, oil, basil, salt and pepper. Pour over vegetables, toss to coat. Serve on lettuce leaves.

CAULIFLOWER SALAD

3 C. cauliflower
½ C. celery
1 green pepper
1 red onion
8 ripe olives
1 jar pimento

6 oz. grated cheddar cheese
Some green olives
8 oz. bottle Caesar salad dressing
1 small container sour cream
2 T. juice from ripe olives

Chop up all vegetables and add sour cream, salad dressing and olive juice. Mix. Serve cold.

CALIFORNIA SALAD

1 large head lettuce
6 small green onions
1 lb. bacon (fried and crumbled)
4 oz. shredded cheddar cheese

1 head cauliflower (flowerettes only)
1 small jar mayonnaise
1 C. sugar

Layer cheese and vegetables with lettuce on bottom. Mix mayonnaise and sugar together until smooth. Pour over salad. Toss only just before serving.

BROCCOLI-CAULIFLOWER SALAD

1 head broccoli
1 head cauliflower
5-6 green onions (more or less to taste)

1 C. (approx.) Miracle Whip salad dressing
1 lb. bacon

Fry bacon until crisp and set aside to cool. Wash broccoli and cauliflower and chop into small pieces (use entire head). Place in large mixing bowl. Chop and add green onions. Mix in Miracle Whip until holds together. Crumble bacon and mix in. (If made ahead of time, bacon should not be added until ready to serve.)

CAULIFLOWER, BROCCOLI SALAD

1 medium head cauliflower
1 medium broccoli
½ C. sliced fresh mushrooms
1 small red onion

1 green pepper
Hidden Valley or any buttermilk
    dressing

Chop cauliflower, broccoli, onion and pepper. Add sliced mushrooms. Toss with Hidden Valley or buttermilk dressing.

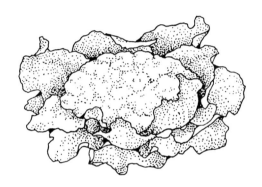

VEGETABLE COMBO

1 head cauliflower (separated into
    flowerettes)
1 bunch broccoli (separated into
    flowerettes)

15 radishes
5 green onions
2 cucumbers (sliced)
2 carrots (sliced)

DRESSING:
1 C. sour cream
1 C. mayonnaise

1 pkg. creamy Italian dressing

Combine dressing and pour over vegetables. Chill.

CAULIFLOWER-BROCCOLI SALAD

1 large head cauliflower
1 large bunch broccoli
1 medium onion
1 C. Miracle Whip
½ C. vegetable oil
⅓ C. vinegar

½ C. sugar
¼ tsp. paprika
1 small can pimentoes (diced)
Dry mustard and pepper to taste
½ tsp. salt

Wash and cut cauliflower, broccoli and onion. Use only tops of cauliflower and broccoli. Mix Miracle Whip, oil, vinegar, sugar, paprika, pimento, mustard, pepper and salt. Pour over vegetables.

BROCCOLI SALAD

1 large head broccoli
1 small can black olives
1 can water chestnuts

1 large white onion
1 bottle zesty Italian salad
dressing

Cut broccoli into bite-size pieces, slice olives and chestnuts, dice onions. Mix together with salad dressing. Refrigerate overnight.

BROCCOLI SALAD

1 head broccoli (chopped)
¼ C. red onions

½ C. golden raisins

DRESSING:
1 C. Miracle Whip
¼ C. sugar

1 T. vinegar

Add dressing to first 3 ingredients, then add ½ C. toasted sunflower seeds or sunflower nuts. Top with bacon crumbs or bacon bits.

OVERNIGHT LETTUCE SALAD

1 head lettuce (cut up)
½ C. chopped celery (more if desired)
1 C. green pepper (chopped)
1 sliced onion
1 pkg. frozen peas (unthawed)

2 C. mayonnaise
2 T. sugar
4 oz. grated cheddar cheese
8 slices bacon (fried and crumbled)

Layer first 5 ingredients in 9x13-inch pans. Spread with mayonnaise, sprinkle with sugar, then cheese and then bacon. Cover with foil and refrigerate overnight. (VARIATION: Sliced or shredded hard cooked eggs may be placed on top of vegetables before mayonnaise is added.)

TASTY SALAD

1 can asparagus soup
5 T. water
1 (3 oz.) pkg. lemon Jello
1 (8 oz.) pkg. cream cheese
 (room temperature)

1 C. chopped green pepper
1 C. chopped celery
½ C. nuts or sliced stuffed olives
½ C. mayonnaise
¼ - ½ C. chopped onions

Heat asparagus soup and water. When hot dissolve lemon Jello in it. Add cream cheese. When this starts to thicken add onion, green pepper, celery, nuts or sliced stuffed olives and mayonnaise. Stir lightly and serve.

CARROT SALAD

2½ lbs. fresh carrots (sliced)
1 onion (cut in rings)
1 green pepper (chopped)
1 tsp. Worcestershire sauce
1 tsp. dry mustard

¾ C. viengar
½ C. oil
1 C. sugar
1 C. undiluted tomato soup

Cook carrots in salted water until tender; drain. Layer carrots, onion and green peppers in a bowl. Blend remaining ingredients together and pour over vegetables.

KRAUT SALAD

1 lb. can sauerkraut (cut up)
1 C. onion (chopped, to taste)
1 C. celery (diced)

1 large green pepper (chopped)
¼ C. vinegar
¾ C. sugar

Make the dressing by boiling the sugar and vinegar until sugar is dissolved. Pour over vegetables while hot. Mix well and store in covered container in the refrigerator.

"SECRET" DILLED CUCUMBERS

3 medium cucumbers
¾ cup white vinegar
¾ cup sugar
1 teaspoon salt
¼ teaspoon white pepper
⅓ cup mayonnaise

¼ cup heavy cream, whipped
⅓ cup sour cream
2 tablespoons dill weed
¼ teaspoon salt
½ teaspoon white pepper

Slice cucumbers *very* thinly; do not peel. Combine vinegar, sugar, 1 teaspoon salt and ¼ teaspoon pepper in a heavy plastic bag. Marinate cucumbers in this for 2 to 3 hours. Remove from bag and press all liquid from cucumbers. Combine mayonnaise, whipped cream, sour cream, dill weed, ¼ teaspoon salt and ½ teaspoon pepper. Add to cucumbers. Chill 3 hours before serving on bed of crisp romaine lettuce. Serves 6 to 8.

WILTED LETTUCE

2 T. sugar
¼ C. bacon drippings (hot)
¼ C. vinegar

¼ C. water
4 slices bacon (cooked)
Large bowl lettuce

Heat sugar, bacon drippings, vinegar and water. Pour over lettuce, stir and crumble cooked bacon on top. Toss.

HOT CHICKEN SALAD

3 cups chicken or turkey,
   chopped
2 10½-ounce cans cream of
   chicken soup
1 cup celery, chopped
4 tablespoons onions, chopped
½ teaspoon salt
Pepper to taste

1 cup mayonnaise
1 cup cracker crumbs
6 hard-cooked eggs, chopped
1 cup slivered almonds
1 teaspoon lemon juice
Chow Mein noodles or grated
   cheese

Mix all ingredients. Top with noodles or grated cheese. Bake at 350 degrees for 30 minutes or until bubbly hot. Serves 12 to 15.

HOT CHICKEN SALAD

3 cups chicken, diced (3 large
   breasts)
2 10½-ounce cans cream of
   chicken soup
2 cups celery, diced
4 tablespoons onion, minced
1 cup mayonnaise

1 cup saltine crackers, crushed
1 cup or 4-ounce package
   slivered almonds
½ teaspoon white pepper
2 tablespoons lemon juice
6 hard-boiled eggs, chopped
⅓ cup pimiento, chopped

Mix ingredients in order listed. Place in a 10-inch casserole and bake at 350 degrees for 40 minutes. Serve plain, in patty shells or on toast. Serves 6 plain, or approximately 16 in patty shells or on toast.

HOT CHICKEN SALAD

2 whole chickens, cooked and
   boned
1 10½-ounce can cream of
   chicken soup
1 10½-ounce can cream of
   mushroom soup
2 cups celery, chopped

2 tablespoons onion, minced
1 teaspoon salt
5 hard-boiled eggs, sliced
1½ cups mayonnaise
Slivered almonds, reserved for
   topping
Potato chips, reserved for topping

Combine all ingredients and toss well. Place in large casserole and top with slivered almonds and potato chips. Bake at 325 degrees for 30 to 40 minutes. Serves 12 to 14.

GERMAN SAUERKRAUT SALAD

1 1-pound can kraut, drained
1 cup celery, chopped
1 medium onion, chopped

1 bell pepper, chopped
1 2-ounce jar pimiento
⅛ cup sugar

Mix and let stand several hours before serving. Serves 8 to 10.

STRAWBERRY FRUIT SALAD

A very fruity fruit salad.

1 quart sliced strawberries
3 large bananas

1 large can diced pineapple
   (29 oz.)
1 lb. small marshmallows (large
   pkg.)

Dressing:

1 cup pineapple juice
juice from 1 lemon
2 eggs

Mix:

1 cup sugar
1 Tbsp. cornstarch
1 pkg. Dream Whip (whipped stiff)

Mix pineapple and marshmallows with dressing and let stand. Just before serving add the strawberries and bananas. Serves 18-20.

OVERNIGHT SLAW

1 large green cabbage, shredded	1 cup oil
1 large Spanish onion, sliced thinly	1 cup vinegar
	1 teaspoon celery seed
1 large bell pepper, diced	1 teaspoon prepared mustard
¾ cup sugar	1 tablespoon salt

Prepare the vegetables and sprinkle with sugar. Combine remaining ingredients except the oil. Bring to a hard boil. Remove from heat and add oil. Pour over vegetables. Refrigerate at least 12 hours. Will keep for 1 week in refrigerator. Serves 8.

Cranberry Fluff

Combine, cover and chill over night:

2 cups raw cranberries, chopped
3 cups tiny marshmallows
¾ cup sugar

Add:

2 cups diced, unpeeled, tart, red apples
½ cup seeded grapes
½ cup broken nut meats
¼ teaspoon salt

Fold in one cup cream, whipped, and ¼ cup mayonnaise. Chill. Makes 8 to 10 servings.

Cranberry Tokay Salad

2 cups fresh cranberries
1 cup Tokay grapes
1 cup pineapple tidbits

1 cup sugar
¼ cup broken walnuts
½ cup cream, whipped

Put cranberries through food chopper, using coarse blade. Stir in sugar and let set over night. Stir, pressing lightly to remove excess juice. Cut grapes in half and remove seeds. Drain pineapple, add grapes, nuts and pineapple to cranberry mixture. Just before serving, fold in whipped cream and garnish with grapes.

Frozen Rhubarb-Cheese Salad

2 cups cottage cheese
2 cups cooked rhubarb
sauce, sweetened

1 teaspoon unflavored gelatin
2 tablespoons cold water
1 cup heavy cream

Sieve the cottage cheese. Measure 2 cups of hot cooked rhubarb and sweeten to taste. Soften the gelatin in the cold water and mix with hot rhubarb sauce. Combine with cottage cheese and chill. Whip cream and fold into chilled mixture. Freeze two hours.

HOT POTATO SALAD

1½ lb. boiling potatoes (sliced)
1 medium onion
6 strips bacon (diced and fried)
⅓ c. vinegar
½ c. water
2 tsp. flour
3 tsp. sugar
1½ tsp. salt
¼ tsp. pepper
½ c. chopped parsley

Boil potatoes with jackets. Peel and slice. Saute diced bacon and onion which has been chopped fine. Add all the other ingredients except parsley and sliced potatoes. Bring to a boil. Add parsley and sliced potatoes. Mix thoroughly. Serve warm or room temperature.

Soup

SOUP

SKINNY CLAM CHOWDER

2 cups water
1 teaspoon salt
2 medium potatoes
2 carrots, diced
1 rib celery, chopped

1 medium onion, minced
1 6½ to 8-ounce can chopped
  clams, undrained
1 cup skim milk

In large saucepan boil water; add salt, potatoes, carrots, celery and onion. Cook 20 minutes or until potatoes and carrots are tender. Add clams and milk; bring to boil. Reduce heat and simmer 5 minutes. Serves 4. 130 calories per serving.

QUICK MEATBALL AND ZUCCHINI SOUP

Meatballs (recipe follows)
1 T. salad oil
1 large onion (slivered)
1 clove garlic (minced)
1 stalk celery (sliced thin)
1 medium carrot (thinly sliced)
1 tsp. basil
¼ tsp. each thyme, oregano

1 (28 oz.) can tomatoes
1 can beef broth (2 C.)
2 C. water
¼ C. tiny soup pasta
3 medium zucchini (1 lb.)
Salt to taste
Grated Parmesan cheese

Brown meatballs in oil in large Dutch oven, removing them as they brown. In same pan, add onion, garlic, celery and carrot. Cook for 5 minutes, stirring occasionally. Sprinkle with basil, thyme and oregano; then add tomatoes (coarsely chopped) and their liquid, broth and water. Return meatballs to pan. Bring to boil, cover, reduce heat and simmer for 30 minutes. Add pasta and cook, covered, boiling gently until pasta is tender (10-15 minutes). Meanwhile, cut zucchini lengthwise into quarters, then slice thinly. Add zucchini to soup and cook, uncovered, until zucchini is just tender, 4-6 minutes. Add salt if needed. Serve with Parmesan cheese to sprinkle over each serving to taste.

MEATBALLS:

1 egg
¼ C. soft bread crumbs
¼ C. grated Parmesan cheese

1 clove garlic (minced)
1 lb. ground beef
¾ tsp. salt

In medium bowl, beat egg, mix in crumbs, cheese, salt and garlic. Lightly mix in ground beef. Shape into 1-inch meatballs.

69

BEEF STEW

1 pkg. cubed stew meat (beef)
1 pkg. carrots
Flour
Sugar to taste

2-3 medium sized onions
8-9 medium potatoes
Salt and pepper to taste

Put some shortening in large pan, flour the cubed beef. Put it in the oil and brown it. Add salt and pepper. When meat is browned and nearly cooked, put 1½-2 T. flour in the pan. Stir well and add water, 2-3 C. Let thicken like gravy. Turn fire off. Dice onions, carrots and potatoes and put them in the gravy with the meat. Salt and pepper some more and add a little sugar. After you get all this together, if you have room, add more vegetables. Add water if it begins to get thick. Cook on low fire until everything is tender. Best way is to cook in a pressure cooker about 45 minutes. If cooked in a regular pan, keep fire low, cook for 3-4 hours. Stir frequently and add water whenever it needs it.

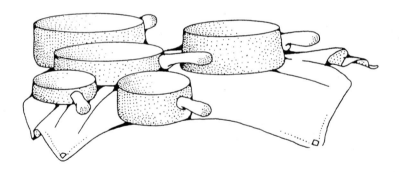

AVOCADO SOUP

1 large avocado
½ cup half and half

1½ cups chicken broth
Garlic salt and pepper to taste

Place all ingredients in a blender and purée. Chill. When serving, garnish with a teaspoon of sour cream and a dash of paprika. Serves 4.

CHICKEN SOUP

5-6 lb. stewing hen	1 diced onion
2 qts. water	2 T. parsley
2 tsp. salt	Salt and pepper to taste
1 C. sliced celery	Noodles (uncooked)
1 C. sliced carrots	

Bring chicken to boil and simmer 2 hours or until chicken is tender. Remove chicken from bone. Add celery, carrots, onions, parsley, salt and pepper to taste. Bring to boil. Simmer 30-45 minutes. Add uncooked noodles and boil until noodles are done, about 10 minutes.

CHICKEN AND NOODLE STEW

1 (1½ C. container) cooked chicken	1 tsp. salt
2 (2 C. containers) chicken broth	½ tsp. poultry seasoning
1 (5⅓ oz.) can (⅔ C.) evaporated milk	1/8 tsp. pepper
½ C. chopped celery	Noodles
½ C. chopped onion	2 T. all-purpose flour
½ C. chopped pimiento	¼ C. cold water

In a large Dutch oven, place frozen cooked chicken and broth. Add evaporated milk. Cook, covered, over medium heat for 15-20 minutes or until thawed. Add chopped celery, onion, pimiento, salt, poultry seasoning and pepper. Bring to boiling, add noodles (homemade if preferred) slowly to boiling broth uncovered, 10-15 minutes. Combine flour and water. Stir into boiling broth. Cook, stirring constantly, until chicken broth mixture is thickened and bubbly. Makes 6 servings.

CREAM OF WATERCRESS SOUP

1½ quarts milk
½ cup celery leaves
¼ cup onion slices
⅙ cup flour
⅙ cup butter

1 tablespoon salt
⅛ teaspoon white pepper
3 bunches watercress, chopped
Optionals: chives, garlic salt,
onion salt

Heat celery leaves and onion slices with milk and strain. Blend flour, butter, salt and pepper and add to hot milk. Stir and cook for 10 minutes. Add watercress and heat thoroughly. Serve immediately with sprinkled chives. Season to taste with garlic salt and onion salt. Serves 12.

CHICKEN AND AVOCADO SOUP

6 cups chicken broth
1 whole chicken breast
2 onions, sliced
½ teaspoon ground coriander
½ teaspoon oregano

½ teaspoon salt
¼ teaspoon black pepper, freshly
ground
1 ripe avocado

Pour the chicken broth into a large saucepan. Add chicken breast, onions and seasonings. Bring to a boil; reduce heat; cover and poach in the simmering broth for 20 minutes. Remove the chicken breast and let it cool. Strain the stock into a saucepan and set it aside. Discard cooked onions. When chicken is cold and firm to the touch, peel off the skin; then, using the sharpest knife you own, cut it into small julienne strips. Just before serving, stir the strips into the soup and heat. Peel the avocado; cut it into slices and add to the soup. The slices will float on top. Serves 6.

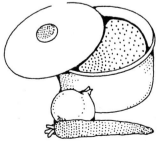

72

Pie

PIE

Best Ever Apple Pie

Cream apple pie is to our family the best apple pie ever made.

Use your own favorite pastry recipe. Peel and slice enough apples to fill crust. Sprinkle apples with ½ teaspoon nutmeg, ½ teaspoon cinnamon and a pinch of salt. Mix together 1 cup sugar, 1 tablespoon flour and ¾ cup sweet thick cream. Pour over apples. Place strips of pie dough over the top. Bake pie in a hot oven at 425 degrees for 10 minutes. Reduce heat to 350 dgrees. Bake until done, from ¾ to 1 hour in all.

Glazed Peach Pie

Prepare and bake 1 pie crust. Slice enough fresh peaches to yield 2½ cups. Sprinkle with 1 tablespoon lemon juice. Add ¼ cup sugar and mix. Set aside for 1 hour.

Drain peaches. Add enough water to juice to make 1 cup. Mix together in a pan ½ cup sugar and 3 tablespoons cornstarch. Cook rapidly, with the juice, until thick and clear. Remove from heat, add ⅛ teaspoon salt and ⅛ teaspoon almond flavoring, also 2 tablespoons butter. Add the peaches. Turn into baked crust and cool. Serve with ice cream or whipped cream. Very good.

Rhubarb Cream Pie

2 tablespoons butter	¼ cup milk or cream
2 cups rhubarb	2 egg yolks
1¼ cups sugar	Salt
2 tablespoons cornstarch	Egg whites for meringue

Melt butter, add rhubarb, and 1 cup sugar. Cook slowly until done. Mix ¼ cup sugar, cornstarch, egg yolks, milk, and salt. Add to rhubarb and cook until thick; pour into baked pie shell and top with meringue.

This is very good in a butter crust:

1 cup flour	1 tablespoon sugar
½ cup butter or margarine	

Mix until crumbly and press in pan. Bake in 350 degree oven until lightly brown.

Cherry Pie

Filling:
Combine 4 tablespoons cornstarch, ¼ cup cherry juice. Add 1 cup honey and beat slowly until thick. Add 3 cups red tart cherries, well drained. Add 1 tablespoon butter. Set aside.

Crust:
Mix ¼ teaspoon salt with 1½ cups flour. Cut in ½ cup cold lard with short, brisk jerks until mixture resembles meal. Add ice water in small portions until you can pick up dough with well floured hands. Divide dough. Roll half out. Spread on 1 tablespoon extra lard, fold edges in. Reroll until ⅛ inch thick or less. Fit into pie tin. Put all cherries in and all juice the pan will hold. Moisten edges, place top dough on, pinch edges, trimming extra dough. Top crust should have design. Sprinkle with sugar and butter. Bake 25 minutes at 450 degrees.

Crumb Topping for Fruit Pie

Mix until crumbly:

> ¼ cup brown sugar (packed)
> ½ cup flour
> ¼ cup soft butter

Use this mixture in place of top pie crust. Bake at 425 degrees 35 to 45 minutes or until nicely browned.

Rhubarb Cream Pie

3 cups rhubarb, diced   ½ teaspoon nutmeg
1½ cups sugar   1 tablespoon butter or
3 tablespoons flour   margarine
2 well beaten eggs

Blend sugar, flour, nutmeg and butter. Add eggs and beat until smooth. Pour over rhubarb which has been placed in a 9 inch pie pan, lined with favorite pastry. Top with pastry, cut in fancy shapes. Bake in hot oven, 450 degrees for 10 minutes; decrease heat to 350 degrees and continue baking for about 30 minutes.

Pumpkin Pie

1 cup pumpkin	1 teaspoon cinnamon
½ cup sugar	½ teaspoon cloves
¼ cup sorghum	½ teaspoon ginger
2 eggs	¼ teaspoon nutmeg
1 cup milk	½ teaspoon salt

Mix pumpkin, sugar, spices and sorghum. Beat egg whites until stiff; add yolks and beat until mixed. Fold into above mixture. Add milk and mix to blend. Pour into unbaked pastry shell; bake 10 minutes at 400 degrees, decrease to 350 degrees and bake 30 minutes more.

Honey Pumkin Pie

2 eggs	½ teaspoon salt
1½ cups pumpkin	¼ teaspoon ginger
¾ cup evaporated milk	1 teaspoon cinnamon
¾ cup honey	¼ teaspoon nutmeg
¼ cup orange juice	¼ teaspoon cloves
¼ teaspoon grated orange rind	1 tablespoon boiling water

Beat the eggs slightly, add pumpkin, evaporated milk, honey, orange juice and rind, salt, and the spices which have been dissolved in boiling water. Pour into unbaked 9 inch pie shell and bake at 425 degrees for 15 minutes, then lower heat to 350 degrees and bake until barely firm, about 25 minutes.

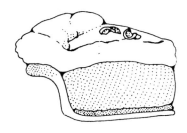

Strawberry Pie

Spread 5 ounces softened cream cheese in bottom of a nine inch baked pie shell. Crush 1 cup strawberries, measure again and add water to make 1 cup.

Mix 1 cup sugar and 3 tablespoons cornstarch. Add to crushed berries and cook until thickened and clear. Add 1 tablespoon butter and a little red food coloring. Put 4 cups fresh berries in pie (whole or halved) and pour sauce over all. Let cool. Serve with whipped cream.

Crunchy Cover for Pumpkin Pie

Blend 1 tablespoon soft butter with 3 tablespoons brown sugar. Add 3 tablespoons coconut and ¼ cup chopped pecans. Sprinkle crumb mixture over pumpkin pie 5 minutes before pie has finished baking.

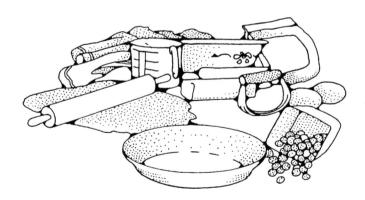

STRAWBERRY PIE

1 qt. fresh strawberries
1 c. sugar
4 T. flour
1 baked pie shell

Mash one-half of the berries thoroughly. Add sugar and flour and blend well. Cook until thick, stirring constantly. Cool. Add remaining berries. Place in baked pie shell just before serving and serve with whipped cream.

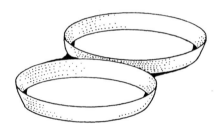

PUMPKIN PIE

1½ C. pumpkin
¾ C. sugar
½ tsp. salt
1 tsp. vanilla

1 tsp. cinnamon
2 eggs (or 3 small eggs)
1¼ C. milk
¾ C. canned evaporated milk

Beat eggs; add vanilla, sugar, salt and cinnamon. Add pumpkin and stir well. Then add milk. Bake at 375° for 40 minutes or until sharp knife inserted in the center comes out clean.

PUMPKIN PIE

2 C. pumpkin	½ tsp. ginger
½ C. sugar	¼ tsp. salt
¼ tsp. nutmeg	7/8 C. milk
½ tsp. cinnamon	1 egg (beaten)

Cook and strain pumpkin or use canned pumpkin. Add spices, salt and milk and heat thoroughly. Stir in egg and pour into pie shell. Bake 5-10 minutes in 450° oven. Turn down to 350° and bake 25-45 minutes until done.

ICE CREAM PUMPKIN PIE

1 C. cooked pumpkin	1/8 tsp. cloves
½ C. brown sugar	¼ tsp. nutmeg
1/8 tsp. salt	1 qt. vanilla ice cream
1 tsp. cinnamon	(softened)

Mix and fill a 9-inch pie shell. Chill for 3 hours.

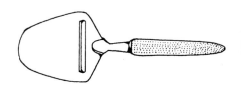

IMPOSSIBLE PUMPKIN PIE

2 eggs	1 tsp. cinnamon
¾ C. sugar	¼ tsp. nutmeg (if you like more
1 (13 oz.) can evaporated milk plus	spicy increase amounts)
enough water to make 2 C.	½ tsp. salt
¼ tsp. cloves	1½ C. pumpkin
½ tsp. ginger	1½ C. biscuit mix

Pour all ingredients into a blender. Blend on medium speed. Pour into a 10-inch greased glass pie plate. Bake at 350° for 40-45 minutes.

80

CRUSTLESS APPLE PIE

Sliced apples	½ cup brown sugar
½ cup (or more) white sugar	1 cup flour
4 tbsp. water	½ tsp. salt
½ cup margarine	

Fill pie tin with sliced apples; sprinkle white sugar on apples. Put water over apples and sugar. Mix until crumbly the rest of the ingredients and sprinkle on top of apples. Bake in moderate oven until apples are done. About 1 hour.

GOOSEBERRY PIE

1 cup sweet cream	1 tbsp. flour
2 egg yolks beaten	2 cups gooseberries
¾ cup sugar	2 egg whites for meringue

Beat egg yolks and sugar with flour, add cream and mix well; pour over gooseberries which have been put in pastry shell. Bake for about 50 minutes, the first 10 minutes at 400°, reduce heat to 300° until custard is set. Gooseberries can be either green or ripe and currants can also be used.

APPLE PIE

6 apples	2 tbsp. flour
¼ tsp. salt	1 tsp. cinnamon
¾ cup sugar	1 tbsp. butter

Pare and slice apples. Sift dry ingredients together and mix with apples. Line pie pan with pastry; fill with apple mixture, dot with butter and cover with top crust. Bake at 375 degrees for 1 hour. 9 inch pie.

NO BAKE RHUBARB PIE

4 cups sliced rhubarb	1 cup cream, whipped
2 cups white sugar	Graham cracker crust
1 pkg. strawberry Jello	

Combine rhubarb and sugar and let stand overnight or until juice comes out. Boil until tender and while hot add jello. Stir until dissolved. Cool until syrupy and fold in whipped cream. Pour into crust and refrigerate until ready to serve.

FRESH STRAWBERRY PIE

1 qt. strawberries	1 tsp. lemon juice
¾ cup water	baked pie shell
1 cup sugar	whipped cream
3 tbsp. cornstarch	

Combine 1 cup of the berries with the water, sugar and cornstarch. Cook until clear; add lemon juice and cool. Put remaining berries in baked shell and pour the glaze over all. Refrigerate. Serve with whipped cream.

Cake

CAKE

APPLE NUT CAKE

Here is a cake which is so good that it "needs no frosting,"

2 cups chopped apples	1 egg	½ cup cooking oil
(unpeeled)	½ cup nuts	1 tsp. vanilla
1½ cups flour	1 cup sugar	½ cup coconut
½ tsp. salt	1 tsp. soda	

Mix apples and sugar. Let stand until juice flows. Sift flour, soda and salt. Add to apples. Add remaining ingredients, and bake at 350° for 40 to 45 minutes.

Rhubarb Cake

1¼ cups sugar	1 teaspoon soda
½ cup vegetable shortening	1 teaspoon cinnamon
2 eggs	¼ teaspoon cloves
½ cup milk	¼ teaspoon salt
2 cups flour	½ teaspoon allspice
	2 cups rhubarb, cut

Cream sugar, shortening and eggs. Sift flour, measure, and add soda, spices and salt to it. Mix well. Stir in rhubarb. Pour into 8"x12" pan and add following topping.

Topping:
⅓ cup brown sugar
½ teaspoon cinnamon
½ cup nuts

Sprinkle over top of batter. Bake at 350 degrees for 30 to 35 minutes.

RAW APPLE CAKE

An exceptionally good cake, simple enough for a rank beginner yet worthy of a gourmet. Easier than apple pie.

4 cups diced apples	2 tsp. vanilla
1¾ cups sugar	2 cups flour
½ cup oil	2 tsp. soda
½ cup nuts	2 tsp. cinnamon
2 eggs, well-beaten	1½ tsp. salt

Mix apples and sugar well and let stand. Sift together flour, soda, cinnamon and salt. Combine all ingredients and place in a 9"x12" pan and bake at 350° for 45 minutes. Use Cream whip topping.

CARROT CAKE

3 C. cake flour
2 C. sugar
2 tsp. cinnamon
1 ½ tsp. soda
1 ½ tsp. salt
1 tsp. baking powder

1 (8 oz.) can crushed pineapple
(save juice)
3 eggs (beaten)
2 tsp. vanilla
1 ½ C. salad oil
2 C. loose grated carrots
1 ½ C. walnuts (chopped)

Combine all dry ingredients. Add pineapple and juice. Add eggs, vanilla, salad oil. Mix well. Add carrots and walnuts. Mix well and pour into greased and floured bundt pan. Bake at 325° for 1 ½ hours. Cool slightly. Remove from pan. Cool completely. Frost or glaze.

PUMPKIN SPICE CAKE

1 ½ C. margarine
1 C. brown sugar
1 C. sugar
4 eggs
2 C. pumpkin
3 C. flour
3 tsp. baking powder

2 tsp. baking soda
1 tsp. salt
2 tsp. cinnamon
1 tsp. pumpkin spice
¼ C. milk
1 C. nuts (opt.)

Cream margarine and sugars until fluffy. Add eggs, beating after each addition. Blend in pumpkin. Add sifted dry ingredients and milk. Add nuts (if desired). Pour into a greased 10-inch tube pan. Bake at 350° for 1 hour. Cool before removing from pan.

ICING:

3 oz. cream cheese (room temp.)
1 (16 oz.) box powdered sugar

1 stick butter or oleo (room temp.)
1 tsp. vanilla

Cream cheese and oleo, add powdered sugar and vanilla.

ZUCCHINI CAKE

3 eggs
1 C. cooking oil
2 C. sugar
2 C. grated zucchini
2 tsp. vanilla
3 C. flour

1 tsp. baking soda
½ tsp. baking powder
1 tsp. salt
3 tsp. cinnamon
½ C. chopped nuts
½ C. raisins (opt.)

Use bundt pan. Preheat oven to 350°. Grease and flour bundt pan. Beat eggs, then add oil, sugar, grated zucchini and vanilla. Cream together. Sift and measure out 3 C. flour, then sift together flour, soda, baking powder, salt and cinnamon. Add sifted ingredients to creamed mixture and mix until thoroughly blended. Add chopped nuts and raisins (opt.). Bake 1 hour. Cool, then sprinkle with powdered sugar if desired.

CHOCOLATE ZUCCHINI CAKE

½ C. + 1 T. butter (soft)
2 C. sugar
3 (1 oz. ea.) squares unsweetened
chocolate (melted)
3 eggs
½ C. milk
2 tsp. orange peel
2 tsp. vanilla

2 C. zucchini (coarsely grated)
2½ C. flour
2½ tsp. baking powder
1½ tsp. baking soda
½ tsp. salt
1 tsp. cinnamon
2 T. powdered sugar
½ tsp. cinnamon

Cream butter, gradually add 2 C. sugar, beating until light and fluffy. Beat in chocolate. Add eggs one at a time, beating well after each addition. Add milk, orange peel, vanilla and zucchini; mix well. Combine flour, baking powder, soda, salt and 1 tsp. cinnamon; add to creamed mixture, mix well. Pour batter into a greased and floured 10-inch bundt pan. Bake at 350° for 1 hour or until toothpick comes out clean. Cool in pan 15 minutes, then remove and complete cooling on wire rack. Combine powdered sugar and ½ tsp. cinnamon, sift over warm cake.

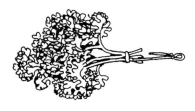

CHOCOLATE ZUCCHINI CAKE

½ C. margarine
1½ C. white sugar
½ C. oil
2 eggs
1 tsp. vanilla
3 C. shredded zucchini

¼ C. milk
2½ C. flour
¼ C. cocoa
1 tsp. soda
1 tsp. salt
½ C. chocolate chips

Combine margarine, sugar, oil, eggs, vanilla and zucchini. Add remaining ingredients. Mix well. Bake in tube pan at 350° for 45-60 minutes. (I bake an extra 15 minutes.)

FROSTING:
½ C. butter or margarine
8 oz. cream cheese

1 tsp. vanilla
2 C. icing sugar

Beat butter and cheese until fluffy. Add vanilla and sugar; mix well. Half of the ingredients for this icing makes plenty for one cake.

RHUBARB CAKE

½ C. oleo
1½ C. sugar
1 egg
½ tsp. salt
1 tsp. baking soda
1 tsp. vanilla

3 C. rhubarb
1 C. milk
2½ C. flour
1 C. brown sugar
½ C. nuts

Mix together oleo, sugar, egg, salt, baking soda, vanilla, milk and flour. Add rhubarb and pour into a greased 9x13-inch pan. Combine 1 C. brown sugar and ½ C. nuts. Sprinkle over top of batter. Bake at 375° for 30-40 minutes.

TOPPING: (Optional)
½ C. oleo
1 C. sugar

½ C. canned milk
1 tsp. vanilla

Mix above ingredients well and pour over cake while still hot.

CINDY'S RHUBARB CAKE

1½ C. sugar
½ C. shortening
1 egg
1 tsp. vanilla
1 C. sour milk
2 C. flour

1 tsp. soda
2 C. raw cut-up rhubarb
½ C. brown sugar
½ tsp. cinnamon
Nuts

Cream together sugar, shortening, egg, vanilla and milk. Add flour and soda. Mix well. Fold in rhubarb. Sprinkle top with brown sugar, cinnamon and nuts. Bake in greased 9x13-inch pan for 50-60 minutes at 325°.

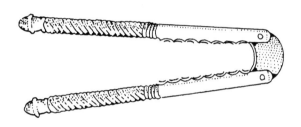

RHUBARB CAKE

2½ C. all-purpose flour
2 tsp. baking powder
1 tsp. salt
1 tsp. cinnamon
1½ C. firmly packed brown sugar
⅔ C. corn oil

1 large egg
1 tsp. vanilla
1 C. milk
1½ C. finely diced rhubarb
1½ C. chopped nuts

Stir together flour, baking powder, salt and cinnamon. In a large bowl stir together sugar, oil, egg and vanilla until blended. Stir in flour mixture in four additions, alternately with milk, just until smooth. Stir in rhubarb and nuts. Bake in a greased and floured 9x13x2-inch pan in a preheated 325° oven, until a cake tester in center comes out clean of batter, about 45 minutes. Cool. Cut in pan. A nut topping is good on top.

SPICE APPLE CAKE

2 cups sugar
1 cup margarine
2 eggs
4 cups chopped apples
1 lemon (juice & grated rind)
1 cup nuts

Bake for 1 hour at 350°.

Sift together:
2 cups flour
1 tsp. soda
1 tsp. salt
1 tsp. nutmeg (level)
2 tsp. cinnamon

ICING

3 ounce pkg. cream cheese
2 cups powdered sugar

½ stick melted butter
1 tsp. vanilla

Combine as usual for frosting.
You may divide this recipe in half for a smaller cake.

Carrot Cake

3 cups carrot, grated raw
4 eggs, unbeaten
2 cups sugar
1½ cups salad oil
2 teaspoons soda

½ teaspoon salt
2 cups flour
1 teaspoon cinnamon
1 teaspoon vanilla
1 cup chopped nuts

In electric mixer bowl, combine carrots, eggs, sugar and oil. Beat until ingredients are mixed. Add remaining ingredients and beat well. Pour into 2 oiled and floured 9 inch pans. Bake at 350 degrees for 40 to 45 minutes. Cool layers.

Put together with one 8 oz. package cream cheese, 1 pound powdered sugar. Soften cheese to room temperature, beat until fluffy and gradually beat in powdered sugar. Add small amount of cream or milk if needed.

Cookies & Bars

COOKIES & BARS

PUMPKIN BARS

2 C. sugar	2 tsp. baking powder
1 C. oil	1-2 tsp. cinnamon
4 eggs	1 tsp. soda
2 C. pumpkin	1 tsp. vanilla
2 C. flour	Chopped nuts (opt.)
½ tsp. salt (opt.)	

Combine sugar, oil, eggs and pumpkin in mixing bowl. Add dry ingredients and mix well. Pour onto ungreased cookie sheet. Bake 20-25 minutes at 350°. Serve plain or sprinkled with powdered sugar or spread cooled cake with cream cheese frosting. (VARIATION: May bake in 2 greased and floured cake pans.)

Apriscotch Bars

Prepare filling as follows. Cook, stirring 1 cup apricot pulp, ½ cup sugar, 1 tablespoon flour, 1 tablespoon lemon juice, 2 tablespoons orange juice, 2 teaspoons butter. Set aside.

Sift together 4½ cups flour, 2 teaspoons cream of tartar, 1 teaspoon soda, 1 teaspoon salt. Cream well 1½ cups brown sugar, ¾ cup vegetable shortening. Add 2 eggs and mix well.

Put ½ the crumbly dough in a greased 9x13-inch pan. Spoon on the filling and sprinkle remaining dough on top. It will spread in baking. Bake in 350 degree oven for 25 to 30 minutes or until brown. Cool slightly. Cut in bars and roll in powdered sugar. May be cut in squares and served with whipped cream as a dessert.

This is an original recipe, tested many times and a winner in a cookie contest.

Pumpkin Cookies

½ cup shortening
1 cup sugar
1 cup strained pumpkin
1 cup raisins
½ cup chopped nuts

2 cups flour
1 teaspoon soda
1 teaspoon baking powder
1 teaspoon vanilla
1 teaspoon cinnamon

Cream shortening and sugar. Add pumpkin, raisins and nuts. Sift and add dry ingredients. Drop from spoon on greased cookie sheet. Bake in 350 degree oven 12-14 minutes. When cool frost with powdered sugar frosting flavored with maple flavoring. These cookies freeze well.

French Apple Cookies

2 cups flour
3 teaspoons baking powder
½ teaspoon salt
1 teaspoon cinnamon
1 teaspoon cloves
½ teaspoon nutmeg

¾ cup shortening
1½ cups brown sugar
1 egg
½ cup milk
1 cup raisins
½ cup nuts

1 cup raw chopped apple

Mix in order given and drop by spoonfuls on cookie sheet. Bake at 375 degrees 12-15 minutes.

Other Desserts

OTHER DESSERTS

RHUBARB TORTE

1 cup flour	¼ tsp. salt
½ cup butter	½ tsp. vanilla
5 tbsp. powdered sugar	¼ cup flour
2 eggs, well beaten	¾ cup chopped nuts (optional)
1½ cups sugar	2 cups cut-up rhubarb
¾ tsp. baking powder	

Combine the first three ingredients and press in buttered 9x13" pan. Bake at 350 deg. for 15 min. Beat eggs and add sifted dry ingredients, nuts and rhubarb. Mix well. Pour over crust and bake 40 to 45 min. at 350 deg. Serve with whipped cream or ice cream.

APPLE CRISP

1 qt. apples	1 cup flour
¾ cup white sugar	1 tsp. cinnamon
¾ cup brown sugar	5 tbsp. butter

Peel and slice apples into buttered 8x12 baking dish. Mix white sugar with the apple slices. Combine brown sugar, flour and cinnamon; cut in the butter as for pie crust. Put over apple mixture and bake about 45 minutes at 350 degrees. Serve with whipped cream or ice cream.

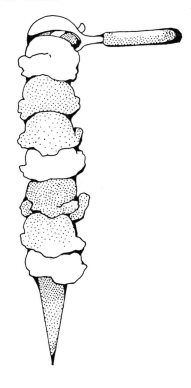

PUMPKIN CHIFFON TORTE

Crust:
1 cup butter

1½ cup flour
2 tbsp. sugar

Mix and pat into 9x13" pan. Bake 15 min. at 375 deg. or until light brown.

Filling:
2 envelopes unflavored gelatin

1 cup cold water

Soak gelatin in water and set aside.

4 egg yolks	1 tsp. nutmeg
2 cups evaporated milk	1 tsp. cinnamon
2½ cups pumpkin	½ tsp. ginger
1½ cups brown sugar	4 egg whites
1 tsp. salt	

In top of double boiler beat egg yolks, stir in milk, pumpkin, 1 cup brown sugar, spices and salt. Cook 10 min., stirring constantly. Remove from heat, add gelatin and stir. Chill in refrigerator until partially set. Beat egg whites and add rest of the brown sugar; fold into gelatin mixture. Pour over crust and refrigerate to complete setting.

RHUBARB STRAWBERRY ROLL

2 cups Bisquick	½ sugar
¾ cup milk	1½ cups sugar
2 cups rhubarb	2 cups water
1 cup strawberries	

Mix the Bisquick and milk. Roll into oblong shape to ⅓ inch thickness. Mix the rhubarb, strawberries and ½ cup sugar; spread over Bisquick mix and roll. Cut in 1½ inch slices. Mix the 1½ cups sugar and water and boil. Pour into buttered 8x8" pan. Place the slices in the syrup. Bake at 450 deg. for 25 to 30 min. Serve with whipped cream.

98

APPLE DELIGHT

8 quartered apples
1 c. sugar
¼ c. butter
¾ c. flour
1 tsp. cinnamon

Slice apples thin and place in buttered dish. Combine rest of ingredients and crumble over top of apples. Bake 350° for 30 minutes.

STRAWBERRY GLAZED CHEESECAKE

Crust:

1⅓ c. fine graham cracker crumbs (about 20 crackers)
¼ c. finely chopped walnuts
½ tsp. cinnamon
½ c. butter, melted

Filling:

3 well-beaten eggs
2 - 8 oz. pkgs. cream cheese, softened
1 c. sugar
¼ tsp. salt
2 tsp. vanilla
½ tsp. almond extract
3 c. dairy sour cream

Glaze:

1 pt. fresh strawberries
1 c. water
1½ T. corn starch
½ c. sugar

For Crust: Mix ingredients and press onto the bottom of 9-inch springfoam pan. Bake at 325° for 10 minutes.

For Filling: Beat cream cheese, sugar, salt, almond and vanilla extract with electric mixer until well blended. Add sour cream; mix well. Add eggs, 1 egg at a time, mixing on low speed after each addition just until blended. Pour into crust. Bake at 325° for 1 hour and 5 minutes or until center is almost set. Loosen cake from rim of pan; cool before removing rim. Refrigerate for 4 hours or overnight.

For Glaze: In a small pan, mix sugar, corn starch and sugar. Cook over low heat, stirring constantly, until thickened. Cool and add strawberries. Spread over chilled cake. Serve.

99

RHUBARB TORTE

2 C. graham cracker crumbs	1½ C. miniature marshmallows
¼ C. melted oleo	1 medium carton frozen whipped
¼ C. sugar	topping
4 C. sliced rhubarb	2 C. milk
3-4 T. cornstarch	1 (3¾ oz.) pkg. vanilla instant
1½ C. sugar	pudding
¾ C. water	

Mix graham crackers, melted oleo and ¼ C. sugar. Reserve 4 T. for topping and press remaining crumbs into 9x13-inch cake pan. Bake 8-10 minutes at 350°. Cool. Cool rhubarb, cornstarch, sugar and water over low heat for 5 minutes. Remove from heat. Add a few drops of red food coloring. Cool. Spoon over crust. Fold marshmallows into whipped topping; spread over rhubarb. Prepare pudding according to package directions; spread over marshmallow mixture. Sprinkle reserved crumbs over top. Chill.

RHUBARB LAYER DESSERT

4 C. rhubarb	1 C. sugar
1 white cake mix	1 pkg. strawberry Jello
1⅓ C. warm water	¼ C. oleo or butter

Put rhubarb in bottom of greased and floured pan, then sugar over rhubarb, then cake mix and the Jello over cake mix and then water and oleo. Bake at 350° for 50 minutes.

Apple Torte

2 eggs	1 teaspoon baking powder
1 cup white sugar	½ teaspoon salt
¼ cup brown sugar	2 medium apples
½ cup flour	1 cup chopped nuts
½ pint cream	

Beat eggs until stiff. Add sugar gradually, continuing to beat. Fold in sifted dry ingredients. Add finely cut apples and nuts. Pour into buttered 9-inch square pan or deep 10-inch pie pan. Bake 25 minutes at 375 degrees. Serve with whipped or ice cream.

RHUBARB ROLLS

2 C. flour
3 tsp. baking powder
¼ tsp. salt
½ C. butter

¾ C. milk
3 C. finely cut rhubarb
1 C. sugar
½ tsp. cinnamon

SYRUP:
1 C. hot water
1 C. sugar

3 T. butter

Mix flour, baking powder and salt. Cut in butter and add milk. Mix lightly. Roll on a floured board into a rectangle shape about 12-inches long. Mix rhubarb, sugar and cinnamon. Spread on dough. Roll dough tightly like a jelly roll and cut into twelve 1-inch sections. Place cut side down on 9x13-inch pan. Make a syrup of 1 C. hot water, 3 T. butter and 1 C. sugar. Pour syrup over rolls and bake 40 minutes or until lightly browned at 350°.

APPLE-CHEDDAR SNACK

1 (4 serving size) pkg. sugar-free
    gelatin (cherry· or any red flavor)
¾ C. boiling water
Ice cubes

½ C. apple or orange juice
¾ C. diced apples
¼ C. shredded cheddar cheese

Dissolve gelatin in boiling water. Add ice cubes to apple or orange juice to make 1¼ C. juice and ice. Add to gelatin, stir until thickened and remove any unmelted ice. Add diced apple and shredded cheese. Pour into dishes. Chill until set, about 30 minutes. Makes about 2 C. or 4 servings. 60 calories per serving.

Apple Torte

2 cups flour
½ cup oatmeal
1 cup brown sugar
3 tablespoons cornstarch
1 cup white sugar
Juice of 1 orange plus
    water to make 1 cup

½ teaspoon cinnamon
½ teaspoon nutmeg
¾ cup shortening
¼ teaspoon salt
1 teaspoon vanilla
1 quart sliced apples, peeled
Grated rind of 1 orange

Method: Mix flour, oatmeal, brown sugar and shortening as for a pie crust. Reserve 1 cup of mixture and pat remaining mixture into a 9-inch pie plate or 8x12-inch cake pan.

Combine the white sugar, salt, cornstarch and orange juice and cook until it thickens. Add vanilla, apples and spices and mix well. Pour into crumb lined pan. Sprinkle with the 1 cup reserved crumbs and bake in 350 degree oven for 45 minutes or until apples are tender. Serve with whipped cream.

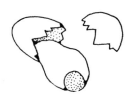

Rhubarb Crisp

Mix together the following ingredients and pour into a shallow glass cake pan 8x8x2-inches.

3 cups cut rhubarb
3 eggs, slightly beaten

1¼ cups sugar
2 tablespoons flour

Sprinkle over this a topping consisting of the following ingredients which are blended together:
⅔ cup brown sugar   ½ cup flour
        3 tablespoons butter

Bake at 350 degrees for about 1 hour. Serve either warm or chilled with whole milk or cream. Also goes very well with ice cream.

Strawberry Swirl

1 cup graham cracker crumbs	1 tablespoon sugar
¼ cup butter or margarine	
2 cups fresh sliced strawberries	2 tablespoons sugar
1 3-ounce package strawberry gelatin	1 cup hot water
½ pound marshmallows	½ cup milk
1 cup whipping cream, whipped	

Mix crumbs, sugar and butter; press firmly over bottom of 9x9x2-inch baking dish. Chill until set.

Sprinkle 2 tablespoons sugar over sliced berries; let stand ½ hour. Drain, reserving juice.

Dissolve gelatin in the 1 cup hot water; add cold water to juice to make 1 cup. Add to gelatin mixture. Chill until partially set.

Meanwhile, combine marshmallows and milk, heat until marshmallows melt. Cool, then fold in whipped cream. Add berries to gelatin, then swirl in marshmallow mixture to marble. Pour into crust. Chill to set. Cut in 9 or 12 squares.

Chilled Raspberry Creme

2 cups vanilla wafer crumbs	1 cup whipping cream
1 cup powdered sugar	½ cup soft butter
½ teaspoon salt	1 teaspoon vanilla
2 pints raspberries (fresh)	2 eggs

Method: Line an 11x7x2-inch glass baking dish with half the crumbs. Cream butter, gradually add sugar. Add vanilla and salt and beat until very fluffy. Add eggs one at a time, beating well after each addition; spread mixture carefully over crumbs on dish. Arrange raspberries over creamed mixture; whip cream and spread over berries. Do not sweeten cream. Sprinkle remaining crumbs over whipped cream. Refrigerate at least 3 hours, preferably over night. Cut in squares and top each square with a berry. (This recipe is very good with fresh strawberries also.)

Quick and Easy Rhubarb Shortcake

Enjoy fresh rhubarb in this quick to bake shortcake.

1 cup sugar	2 cups flour
1 cup sour cream	Pinch of salt
1 teaspoon soda	Dash of nutmeg

2 cups fresh rhubarb, cut up

Mix sugar and cream together, add soda and stir. Stir in flour and rhubarb. Spread in a greased pan. Sprinkle with nutmeg. Bake at 350 degrees for 30 minutes. Serve warm with cream.

Note: We like it cold too. I use sweet or sour cream.

APPLE NUT CRUNCH DESSERT

A delight to serve — and to eat.

1 egg	¾ cup sugar
2 Tbsp. flour	1¼ tsp. baking powder
⅛ tsp. salt	½ cup chopped nuts
½ cup raw, chopped apples	1 tsp. vanilla

Beat egg and sugar until very smooth. Mix flour, baking powder and salt, then stir into the sugar-egg mixture. Add apples, nuts and vanilla. Bake in a buttered pie pan or square pan in a medium oven (350°) for 35 minutes. Serve with whipped cream or ice cream.

EASY FRUIT COBBLER

1 stick butter	1 cup milk
1 cup self-rising flour	1 quart fruit
1 cup sugar	

In oven melt butter in 2-quart dish. In a bowl mix flour and sugar. Add melted butter and milk. Stir until smooth. Pour fruit into dish in which butter was melted. Pour batter over fruit. Bake at 350 degrees for 40 minutes. Serves 6.

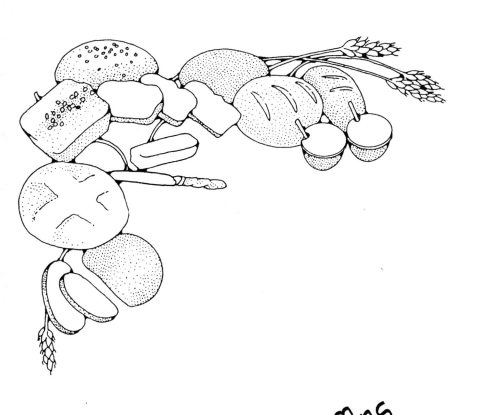

Breads, Rolls, Muffins

BREAD

RHUBARB BREAD

A moist springtime treat.

1½ cups brown sugar	1 tsp. vanilla
⅔ cup liquid shortening	2½ cups flour
1 egg	1 tsp. baking soda
1 cup sour milk	1½ cups finely diced rhubarb
1 tsp. salt	
½ cup chopped nuts (optional)	

For topping: ½ cup white sugar, 1 tsp. cinnamon, 1 Tbsp. melted butter.

Combine brown sugar and shortening. Stir in egg and sour milk with vanilla. Add sifted dry ingredients. Stir in rhubarb and nuts. Pour mixture into two bread pans. Combine topping ingredients and sprinkle on top of batter. Bake 40 minutes at 325°. DO NOT OVER BAKE.

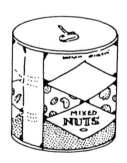

PECAN TARTS

2 sticks margarine
½ pound cream cheese
2¼ cups flour

¼ teaspoon salt
¾ cup pecans, ground

SYRUP:

1 pound box brown sugar
2 tablespoons butter, melted

3 eggs, beaten
¾ teaspoon vanilla

Mix softened margarine and cream cheese. Add salt and flour. Mix and chill dough ½ hour. Roll into balls (walnut size) and put in small muffin tins. Press with thumb to make tart shell. Place ¼ teaspoon ground nuts on bottom of each tart shell. Add 1 teaspoon syrup to each. To prepare syrup, combine brown sugar, butter, eggs and vanilla and put in each tart. Bake at 350 degrees for 20 minutes. Remove shells from muffin tins immediately after taking from oven. Sprinkle with powdered sugar when cool. Makes 60 small tarts or 30 larger ones.

ZUCCHINI BREAD

A moist bread with the taste of summertime.

4 **eggs**	1 **tsp. vanilla**
2 **cups sugar**	1¼ **tsp. baking soda**
1 **cup vegetable oil**	1 **tsp. salt**
3½ **cups unsifted flour**	1 **cup nuts**
¾ **tsp. baking powder**	2 **cups peeled & grated zucchini**
1 **tsp. cinnamon**	

Beat eggs in a large bowl. Add sugar gradually, then add vegetable oil. Add other ingredients to mixture and layer alternately with zucchini. Bake at 350° for 50-55 minutes in one loaf pan and one bundt pan.

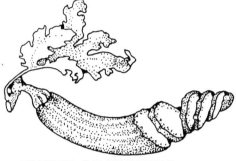

QUEEN OF MUFFINS

Here's a recipe worthy of its name with enough variations to make it a reoccuring surprise.

¼ **cup melted butter**	1½ **cups sifted all-purpose flour**
1 **egg well beaten**	½ **tsp. salt**
2½ **tsp. baking powder**	¾ **cup blueberries**
½ **cup milk**	
⅓ **cup sugar**	

Cream butter and sugar, add egg and blend. Sift dry ingredients and add alternately with milk. Mix only to combine. Fold in blueberries with the last amount of flour.

Bake in greased pans at 400° for 20 minutes or until done.

Yield: 12 muffins.

For variations use crushed pineapple, chopped red sour cherries, bacon bits, raisins, apricots or chopped uncooked prunes.

PEACH PANCAKES

This batter works well with all kinds of fruits and for corn pancakes, too.

2½ cups all-purpose flour	**4½ tsp. baking powder**
4½ tsp. sugar	**½ tsp. salt**
3 eggs	**2 cups milk**
¼ cup melted butter	**1 cup chopped peaches—well drained**

Sift dry ingredients. Beat the eggs and add milk. Add milk and egg mixture to dry ingredients stirring only enough to combine. Add melted butter. Fold in the fruit.

Heat ⅛ inch melted fat in skillet. Spoon batter carefully into the hot fat. (Once-third cup of batter makes a three inch pancake.) Fry until brown on one side, turn and fry until done. Drain on paper toweling.

Yield: 12 pancakes.

Hint: Other fresh, frozen or canned fruits may be used. Be sure the fruit is well-drained.

The same batter may be used with corn or cooked rice.

HEALTH BREAD

A quick bread that's a meal in itself.

6 cups whole wheat flour	3 cups shredded raw carrots
1 cup wheat germ	2 pounds raisins
1 tsp. salt	1 cup soybean oil
3 tsp. baking powder	2 cups warm milk
⅔ cup brown sugar	2 tsp. cinnamon

Mix dry ingredients together. Mix wet ingredients together. Then add all together. Place in oiled loaf pans and bake for 1 hour at 350°. Makes 3 loaves.

ZUCCHINI BREAD

4 eggs
2 C. sugar
1½ tsp. soda
¾ tsp. baking powder
1 tsp. vanilla
1 C. raisins (opt.)

1 C. oil
3½ C. flour
½ tsp. salt
1 tsp. cinnamon
2 C. grated zucchini
½ C. nuts (opt.)

Mix eggs, oil, sugar, vanilla and zucchini together. Add all to dry ingredients. Pour into greased pans. Bake on lowest rack in oven at 350° for 55 minutes. Makes two 9x5x2-inch loaves.

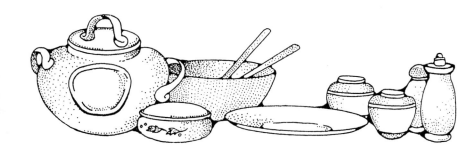

ZUCCHINI BREAD WITH PINEAPPLE

3 eggs
1 tsp. vanilla
1 (8 oz.) can crushed pineapple
2 tsp. baking powder (drained)
¾ C. walnuts
1 tsp. salt

1 C. oil
2 C. zucchini
2 C. sugar
3 C. flour
1½ tsp. cinnamon

Mix all ingredients well. Pour into 2 greased loaf pans and bake at 350° for 1 hour.

112

ZUCCHINI BREAD

1½ C. flour
1 tsp. cinnamon
½ tsp. baking soda
½ tsp. salt
½ tsp. nutmeg
¼ tsp. baking powder

1 C. sugar
1 C. shredded unpeeled zucchini
1 egg
¼ C. cooking oil
¼ tsp. lemon peel
½ C. walnuts

Mix flour, cinnamon, soda, salt, nutmeg and baking powder. Beat sugar, zucchini and egg. Add oil and lemon peel. Stir flour mix into zucchini mix. Add nuts. Pour into greased loaf pan. Bake at 350° for 55-60 minutes.

PUMPKIN BREAD

3 C. flour
2 tsp. baking soda
1 tsp. nutmeg
1 tsp. cinnamon
½ tsp. salt
3 C. sugar

1½ C. pumpkin
4 eggs
⅔ C. water
1 C. vegetable oil
Nuts or raisins (opt.)

Mix together all ingredients with mixer. Pour into greased bread pans. Bake at 350° for 1 hour or less.

CARROT BREAD

2 C. flour
1 tsp. baking soda
1 tsp. cinnamon
½ tsp. nutmeg
3 eggs

1¼ C. sugar
¼ C. vegetable oil
1¼ C. grated carrots
½ C. milk
¼ C. chopped nuts

Combine flour, soda, cinnamon and nutmeg in a small bowl and set aside. In a large mixing bowl beat eggs and sugar. Add oil and mix well. Mix in grated carrots and milk. Slowly add flour mixture a little at a time, beating well after each addition. Stir in nuts. Grease 9x5x2-inch loaf pan. Pour batter in and bake at 375° for 40-50 minutes.

114

CRANBERRY ORANGE NUT BREAD

¾ C. sugar
1 egg
1 ¼ C. orange juice
1 T. grated orange rind

3 C. Bisquick
¾ C. chopped nuts
1 C. chopped cranberries

Heat oven to 350°. Mix sugar, egg, orange juice, rind and Bisquick. Beat vigorously 30 seconds. Batter may still be lumpy. Stir in nuts and berries. Pour into well greased loaf pan. Bake 55-60 minutes, toothpick inserted in center should come out clean. Crack in top is typical. Remove from pan. Cool before slicing.

Spicy Apple Muffins

2 cups flour
¼ cup sugar
½ teaspoon salt
4 teaspoons baking powder

½ teaspoon cinnamon
1 egg, beaten
¼ cup melted shortening
1 cup milk

1 cup finely cut raw apple that has been sweetened with ¼ cup sugar

Combine sifted dry ingredients with liquid, adding sweetened apples last. Bake 20-25 minutes in 425 degree oven.

ZUCCHINI PANCAKES

½ C. flour
2 C. shredded zucchini
¾ tsp. salt

1/8 tsp. pepper
2 eggs (separated)
Oil for frying

In small bowl mix flour, zucchini, salt, pepper and egg yolks. In another bowl, beat egg whites until stiff but not dry. Fold into zucchini mixture. Drop by heaping tablespoons into hot fat. Brown on both sides. Drain. Serve immediately.

Misc.

MISC.

118

MOTHER'S RHUBARB MARMALADE

7 C. sugar
7 C. finely chopped rhubarb

3 large oranges (chopped fine)
Rind from one orange (chopped
or shredded fine)

Mix the above together. Let stand overnight. The following morning in a large kettle boil hard for about ½ hour, stirring occasionally. Skim and put in glass jars. Seal or refrigrate.

CHILI SAUCE

1 gal. peeled and quartered ripe
   tomatoes
4 large onions (chopped)
4 large green peppers
1 qt. vinegar
1 T. ground ginger

1 T. cinnamon
1 T. salt
1 tsp. salt
1 tsp. cloves
2 C. sugar

Boil all ingredients until thick. Can using accepted methods. Great on meat.

PEAR BUTTER

2 qts. pear pulp (about 20 medium)
4 C. sugar
1 tsp. grated orange rind

⅓ C. orange juice
½ tsp. ground nutmeg

To prepare pulp: Quarter and core pears. Cook until soft, adding only enough water to prevent sticking. Press through a sieve or food mill. Measure pulp. Add remaining ingredients; cook until thick, about 15 minutes as mixture thickens. Stir frequently to prevent sticking. Pour hot into hot Ball jars leaving ¼-inch head space. Adjust caps. Process pints and quarts 10 minutes in boiling water bath at simmering temperature (180°-185°). Cool. Test for seal. Store. Yield about 2 pints.

STRAWBERRY BUTTER

1 pint fresh strawberries

½ pound unsalted butter

1 cup powdered sugar (If using fresh berries, add ½ cup sugar.)

Put ingredients in blender in order given. Blend until creamy and smooth. If the mixture appears to curdle, continue blending until creamy. Chill. Serve with toast, biscuits, muffins, pancakes or waffles. Makes 2½ cups.

Ozark Pudding

2 eggs

1½ cups sugar

¾ cup flour

2½ teaspoons baking powder

¼ teaspoon salt

1 cup chopped nuts (may be omitted)

2 cups raw chopped apples

2 teaspoons vanilla

Beat eggs and add sugar. Add dry ingredients and mix well. Stir in nuts, apples and vanilla. Pour into buttered pan and sprinkle with cinnamon. Bake in 350 degree oven for 45 minutes.

Rhubarb or raw peaches may be used in place of apples but omit cinnamon.

GRAPE JAM

Concord grapes; any amount. Squeeze skins off grapes and cook pulp until seeds are loose. Strain. Add skins to juice and boil 3 minutes. Measure and add 1½ cups sugar to each cup of fruit. Do not cook after sugar has been added. Stir real well every little while. Put in sterilized jars in the morning.

SWEET PICKLE RELISH

8 C. cucumbers
4 C. onion
2 green peppers
2 red peppers
½ C. pickling salt

7 C. sugar
4 C. cider vinegar
2 T. celery seed
2 T. mustard seed

Grind cucumbers, onions and peppers. Stir in pickling salt. Cover with water and let stand 2 hours. Drain. Heat to boiling sugar, vinegar, celery seed and mustard seed. Add vegetables and simmer 10 minutes. Pack in pint jars and seal and put in water bath for 10 minutes.

PICKLE RINGS

7 lbs. cucumbers
2 C. pickle lime
8½ C. water
10 C. sugar
6 oz. cinnamon red hots
8 broken cinnamon sticks
1 C. white vinegar

1 small bottle red coloring
1 T. alum
2 C. white vinegar
2 C. water
10 C. sugar
6oz. cinnamon red hots

Cut cucumbers in rings. Soak cucumber rings in lime and water for 24 hours. Rinse and drain. Put 1 C. vinegar, red hots, alum and pour water to cover. Simmer 2 hours. Drain and heat 2 C. white vinegar, 2 C. water, 10 C. sugar, 6 oz. cinnamon red hots, and 8 broken cinnamon sticks. Bring to a boil. Pour over cucumbers. Let stand overnight. Next day drain. Bring mixture to a boil. Pour over rings again. Next day put in jars. Boil sugar mixture. Pour over cucucmbers in jars and seal. These resemble spiced apple rings.

GREEN TOMATO PICKLES

4 lbs. green tomatoes
4 medium onions (diced)
1 C. green peppers (diced)
8 C. white vinegar

5 C. sugar
¼ C. mustard seed
1 T. celery seed
1 tsp. ground turmeric

Wash and cut small green tomatoes (cut into chunks, not peeled). Place even amount into 8 pint jars. Add onion and pepper into jar in equal amounts. Mix remaining ingredients in saucepan. (Spices can be tied in bag.) Bring to a boil. Pour over tomatoes. Adjust lids. Process in boiling water bath 15 minutes.

BEET PICKLES

1 C. water   1 C. vinegar
1 C. sugar   Salt

Pack hot beets in warm sterilized jars and pour the hot syrup over beets (made from the ingredients above).

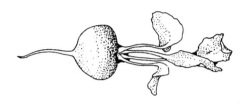

PICKLED NOODLES

1 pkg. noodles   ½ C. chopped onion
1 T. oil   ½ C. chopped cucumber
1½ C. vinegar   ½ C. chopped green pepper
2 C. sugar   ½ C. chopped carrots
1 tsp. garlic salt   ½ C. chopped celery
1 T. yellow mustard

Cook noodles as directed. Drain and coat with 1 T. oil. Blend vinegar, sugar, garlic salt and mustard until well mixed. Add to noodles. (You may add ½ C. of any or all of the chopped vegetables listed.) Mix well and refrigerate overnight or 2-3 hours before serving. Keeps a very long time in the refrigerator.

LAZY HOUSEWIFE PICKLES

1 onion   1 T. salt
4 cucumbers   ½ tsp. turmeric
1½ C. sugar   ½ tsp. celery seed
1½ C. vinegar   ½ tsp. mustard seed

Slice cucumbers and onion in a quart jar. Combine remaining ingredients. Mix thoroughly (do not heat). Pour cold mixture over cucumbers. Store in refrigerator. Ready to eat in 5 days.

RAW TOMATO RELISH

12½ lbs. ripe tomatoes	1 C. salt
3 onions	1 qt. onions
1 hot pepper	6 C. sugar
3 green peppers	2 oz. mustard seed
3 stalks celery	½ C. horseradish

Grind tomatoes, onions, peppers and celery. Add salt and place in bag in drain overnight. Make syrup of vinegar and sugar. Boil and cool. In the morning add syrup to tomatoes with mustard seed and horseradish. Stir and put cold in jars. Store in refrigerator or may be frozen.

CRISP SLICED PICKLES

1 gal. (4-inch or 5-inch) pickles	1 tsp. ginger
1 C. salt	1 qt. vinegar
1 T. alum	5 C. sugar
1 tsp. celery seed	1 tsp. msutard seed

Slice cucumbers thin; do not remove peeling. Cover with water to which salt has been added. Let stand 7 days stirring each day. On the 8th day, drain and rinse. Cover with boiling water and alum. Bring to a boil; drain and rinse. Cover with boiling water and ginger. Let stand 2 hours. Drain and cover with vinegar, sugar, celery seed and mustard seed. Bring to a boil. Pack and seal.

GREEN TOMATO SWEET PICKLES

4 C. (heaping) sliced green tomatoes	1 T. mustard seed
4 onions (size of a dollar)	1 tsp. whole cloves
2 sweet red peppers	1 inch stick cinnamon (crushed)
2 C. vinegar	2 T. salt
1 C. sugar	

Combine sliced green tomatoes and sliced onions. Mix with 2 T. salt. Weight down. Let stand 2 hours. Drain. Rinse in cold water and drain again. Combine vinegar, sugar and spices. Bring to the boiling point and let boil gently for 5 minutes. Add tomatoes and onions. Simmer until onions are clear looking. Pour boiling hot into sterilized jars. This will average enough for a quart jar unless you have a great deal of shrinkage from over cooking. With this recipe as a guide you can make up as many quarts as you wish.

EASY PICKLES

1 C. vinegar
Water
1½ tsp. salt

1 tsp. pickling spice
½ tsp. alum

Fill quart jar with cucumbers. Add 1 C. vinegar and finishing filling with cold water. Add salt and spices. Add green color if desired. Seal cold. To use, at least 6-8 weeks later, wash well (throw away vinegar and spices). Add to split cucumbers 1 C. sugar and ¼ C. water, mix and turn for few days to ripen. These are delicious and are so quick to can in busy summertime.

PICKLED PASTA

1 lb. box mostaccioli (or other pasta)
1½ C. vinegar
1½ C. sugar
2 T. prepared mustard
1 tsp. garlic powder

1 tsp. salt
1 tsp. coarse pepper
1 T. parsley
1 medium onion
1 medium cucumber (peeled)

Cook pasta to desired doneness and drain. Toss with small amount of oil to prevent sticking. Place remaining ingredients in blender or food processor and blend. Toss with pasta and refrigerate overnight. This looks like too much dressing, but pasta will absorb liquid as it marinates. Will keep several weeks.

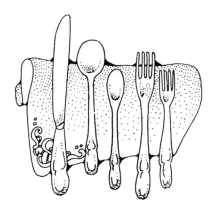

FROZEN FRUIT

1 (10 oz.) pkg. frozen strawberries
1 (6 oz.) can frozen orange juice
1 (6 oz.) can frozen lemonade
1 can medium crushed pineapple
and use juice also

2 C. water
½ C. sugar
3-6 medium sized bananas
(sliced)

Mix all of fruit together. Put in 3 oz. containers and freeze.

FROZEN CUCUMBERS AND ONIONS

3 qts. fresh cucumbers
2 lbs. onions (sliced)
2 red peppers
2 green peppers

1 bunch celery (sliced)
½ C. pickling salt
6 C. sugar
4 C. vinegar

Slice 3 quarts fresh cucumbers and 2 lbs. sliced onions. Slice red and green peppers. Slice 1 bunch celery. Cover with mixture of water and ¼ c. pickling salt and let stand overnight. Then drain. Mix sugar and vinegar and stir until dissolved. Pour over vegetables. Put in freezer containers and freeze. Will keep indefinitely.

RHUBARB JAM

8 C. chopped rhubarb   6 oz. pkg. strawberry Jello
4 C. sugar

Combine rhubarb and sugar and bring to a boil. Cook until tender. Remove from heat and add gelatin. Refrigerate or seal. Freezes well too. Can substitute fruit to strawberries.

FROZEN PEARS

1 small can frozen orange juice   1½-2 C. sugar
Fresh Bartlett pears   ⅔ C. water

Cut fresh Bartlett pears into freezer containers. Cut as small or large as you wish. Stir together orange juice, sugar and water. Pour orange juice mixture over pears in containers. Freeze. Serve later with sliced bananas, peaches, grapes or other fruit. Be sure to cover all of pears with orange juice mixture or pears will discolor.

FREEZER PICKLES

3 qts. sliced cucumbers   3 C. sugar
2 onions   1 C. vinegar
2 T. salt   ½ tsp. celery seed

Cover with water and soak 2 hours. In the meantime mix 3 C. sugar, 1 C. vinegar and ½ tsp. celery seed. Heat until sugar is dissolved. Cool. Add to drained cucumbers and freeze. Must be frozen to be good.

ZUCCHINI RELISH

10 C. coarsely ground zucchini   2½ C. vinegar
4 C. onions (chopped fine)   6 C. sugar
5 T. salt   2 T. celery salt
1 red pepper (chopped; I use   1 tsp. turmeric
   1 medium size jar pimiento)   1 tsp. dry msutard
1 green pepper (chopped)

Mix zucchini, onions and salt. Let stand overnight. Wash and drain. Add remaining ingredients and simmer 20 minutes. Pack into sterilized jars and seal.

CORN COB JELLY

12 corn cobs (broken up)   3 C. sugar
4 C. water   1 box Sure-Jell

Boil broken up corn cobs in 4 C. water for 30 minutes. Drain off the juice in a sieve or sock or strainer. Add sugar and Sure-Jell to the juice and boil for 3 minutes. Put in jars and seal with paraffin.

FRUIT COCKTAIL MIX

4 C. sugar   2 cantaloupes (cut in chunks
2 qts. water   or balls)
1 (6 oz.) can frozen orange juice 2 honeydew melons (chunks
1 (6 oz.) can frozen lemonade   or balls)
1 watermelon (cut in chunks or balls) 3 lbs. white grapes
3 lbs. peaches (cut in chunks)

Mix melons and fruit and put into freezer containers. Mix sugar and water and bring to a boil stirring constantly. Stir in frozen orange juice and lemonade and pour over mixed fruit and melons. Freeze. Use within 6-8 months.

CREAMED STYLE CORN

24 C. corn   ½ C. salt
3 C. sugar   8 C. water

Cut corn (raw) off cob, going only half kernel deep. Scrap cob. Add other ingredients and cook until hot. Kernels are almost clear in color. Put into containers when cooled. Freeze. Delicious.

FREEZING CORN

5 C. corn   1 C. water
¼ C. sugar   1 C. ice cubes
1 tsp. (scant) salt

Stir together until ice melts. Pack in containers and freeze.

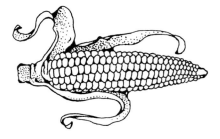

IOWA FREEZING CORN

4 qts. fresh corn   4 tsp. salt
1 qt. water   1 stick oleo
1 C. sugar

Mix first 4 ingredients and bring to a boil. Turn heat down and cook 20 minutes, stirring occasionally. Remove from heat and add oleo. Cool to room temperature. Pack and freeze. Tastes like fresh corn.

VEGETABLE PICKLE

4 cucumbers (cut each into quarters lengthwise and remove pulp. Cut each quarter into 1½ inches lengths and slit each piece three-quarter way up from one end)

1 c. small onions, skinned and cut into four, halfway up from the pointed end

1 c. cauliflower, cut into small pieces

1 large carrot (skinned and cut into 1½ inches length, each length halved and then coarsely sliced)

6 fresh red and 6 green peppers, slit in two up to stem

2 T. finely shredded fresh ginger

*1 serai bulb, 1½ inch from root, cut into 4

8 T. sugar and 2 dessertspoons salt

2 c. white vinegar

Ingredients to be finely ground: 4 slices langkuas, 6 cloves garlic, 1 pc. of very yellow turmeric. Method: put all cut vegetables and the shredded ginger in a flat cane basket and dry in the sun all day. Heat oil in pan. Fry ground ingredients till crisp and fragrant. Add serai, vinegar, salt and sugar to suit your taste. After the mixture has boiled, pour it into a porcelain or pyrex bowl to cool. Put in all vegetables, mix well and keep overnight. This pickle should be made the day before you want to use it. It will keep for about three days and even longer if kept in a refrigerator.
*optional

BEET RELISH

1 qt. boiled and chopped beets	½ tsp. pepper
1 qt. raw chopped cabbage	1 small pinch red pepper
1 cup grated horseradish	1 tbsp. salt
2 cups sugar	

Mix all together, cover with vinegar and let come to a boil. Put in hot jars and seal.

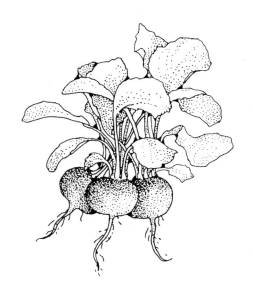

COPPER PENNIES

4 C. pared, thin sliced carrots	1 C. sugar
1 green pepper (cut in strips)	¾ C. vinegar
1 medium onion (cut in rings)	1 tsp. dry mustard
10½ oz. can condensed tomato soup	1 tsp. Worcestershire sauce
½ C. salad oil	½ tsp. salt
¼ tsp. pepper	

Cook carrots in small amount of salted water just until tender-crisp. In plastic container with cover, layer the vegetables. Combine remaining ingredients for marinade and pour over vegetables. Cover and refrigerate. Keeps several weeks.

Need A Gift?

For

- Shower • Birthday • Mother's Day •
  - Anniversary • Christmas •

Turn Page for Order Form
(Order Now While Supply Lasts!)

To Order Copies

Please send me _____copies of Farmers'
Market Cookbook at $9.95 each plus $3.50
S/H for first book and $1.50 thereafter.
Make checks payable to **QUIXOTE PRESS**.

Name _____

Street _____

City _____ State _____ Zip _____

QUIXOTE PRESS
3544 Blakslee St.
Wever, IA 52658
800-571-2665

- -

To Order Copies

Please send me _____copies of Farmers'
Market Cookbook at $9.95 each plus $3.50
S/H for first book and $1.50 thereafter.
Make checks payable to **QUIXOTE PRESS**.

Name _____

Street _____

City _____ State _____ Zip _____

QUIXOTE PRESS
3544 Blakslee St.
Wever, IA 52658
800-571-2665